ARMOR UP
WITH GOD WE DEMOLISH STRONGHOLDS

Jill Deville

SHOW WHAT YOU KNOW

Jill Deville

ISBN 979-8-9878998-7-8 (Paperback)
ISBN 979-8-9878998-8-5 (Hardcover)
ISBN 979-8-9878998-9-2 (Digital)

Copyright © 2023 Jill Deville
All Rights Reserved
First Edition

All rights reserved. No part of this publication may be reproduced, distributed, or transmitted in any form or by any means, including photocopying, recording, or other electronic or mechanical methods without the prior written permission of the publisher. For permission requests, solicit the publisher via the address below.

Jill L Deville
P.O. BOX 876
Basile, La 70515
JillDevilleWorldMinistry@gmail.com
www.JillDevilleWorldMinistry.com

DEDICATION

I dedicate this book to everyone in my life that has been loving, kind, supportive, hate filled, and unsupportive. You have all genuinely helped me to see God's power and authority in and for me! It is one thing to show who you are in Christ, when all is going your way. But rest assured, it is revealing to see who you are in Christ when things are a mess, and you are growing in it. I pray this book will assist many readers to learn how to Show What You Know.

Author, Jill Deville

Jill Deville

2 Corinthians 10:4 NIV ⁴The weapons we fight with are not the weapons of the world. On the contrary, they have divine power to demolish strongholds.

CONTENTS

Introduction		7
Chapter 1:	Buckle the Belt of Truth	15
Chapter 2:	Put on the Breastplate	26
Chapter 3	Fit your Feet in Peace	41
Chapter 4	Take up the Sheild of Faith	53
Chapter 5	Your Helmet of Salvation	66
Chapter 6	Use Your Sword	76
Chapter 7	Armor Up	90
Chapter 8	Activate Your Weapons	95
Chapter 9	Holy Spirit Activate	106
Chapter 10	Show What You Know	129
About the Author		139
Other Titles		141

Jill Deville

INTRODUCTION

Have you ever wondered, "why does my thoughts sometimes go right to the weirdest, meanest, craziest, judgmental, fearful, pitiful, prideful thoughts?" Have you ever wondered why we learn and know God's word; however, our actions and reactions do not reveal that we know or believe God's word ?

In offense, we have defense. In rejection, we retreat to pity or anger. In betrayal, we resort to unforgiveness, and hate. In financial changes or loss, we begin to control, or blame. If medical or mental we run to the hospital, doctor, or medication. Does this sound familiar? The Apostle Paul shared this very thing when he said:

Romans 7:15 NIV I do not understand what I do. For what I want to do I do not do, but what I hate I do.

Paul was truthful with himself and to God. Many Christians do not want to admit they have flaws, sin, or need to work on things. Things that are not of God. Instead of using the armor God gave us, we resort to the weapons that the devil gave us. These weapons look like hate, anger, worry, control, enabling, pride, gossip, complaining, slander, pity, selfishness, unforgiveness, and manipulation. These are powered by fear. The devil has you believing they give you power.

You may not ever admit that, but your actions and reactions reflect That. They reflect that you do believe in those weapons more than God's weapons.

When we resort to the weapons from the devil, we are telling God that we do not need Him, that His promises are not true to us. That His promises, His weapons, His sacrifice, His power is not enough for us. We resort to the creature and not the Creator.

Romans 1:25 NLT They traded the truth about God for a lie. So they worshiped and served the things God created instead of the Creator himself, who is worthy of eternal praise! Amen.

Now that you hearing this, ask yourself why do I trust in myself, others, my work, or the devil, over God? Ask what has convinced you to have so much trust in the creature, or the creation and not the Creator? It starts with your generation, traditions, fitting in, lack of patience, lack of knowledge, lack of faith and control. Until now, you may have never considered or realized that you do not seek God, believe in God, or trust in God first. Until now, you may not have realized that you always jump ahead of God, or put other people, places, or things before God. For most of us, we would never admit it, consider it, or think that we do it. Our actions and reactions show what and who we trust in.

This book will help you to identity the true enemy in our lives is not the person, place or thing that has come against us. Those people, places, and things are of the world and are vessels only. You see each of us is a vessel. Therefore, if we are aware that the fight is not of the flesh but of the spirit, then we will realize only the weapons of the spirit can fight that spirit.

2 Timothy 2: 14- 26 NIV 14 Keep reminding God's people of these things. Warn them before God against quarreling about words; it is of no value, and only ruins those who listen. 15 Do your best to present yourself to God as one approved, a worker who does not need to be ashamed and who correctly handles the word of truth. 16 Avoid godless chatter, because those who indulge in it will become more and more ungodly. 17 Their teaching will spread like gangrene. Among them are Hymenaeus and Philetus, 18 who have departed from the truth. They say that the resurrection has already taken place, and they destroy the faith of some. 19 Nevertheless, God's solid foundation stands firm, sealed with this inscription: "The Lord knows those who are his," and, "Everyone who confesses the name of the Lord must turn away from wickedness." 20 In a large house there are articles not only of gold and silver, but also of wood and clay; some are for special purposes and some for common use. 21 Those who cleanse themselves from the latter will be instruments for special purposes, made holy, useful to the Master and prepared to do any good work. 22 Flee the evil desires of youth and pursue righteousness, faith, love, and peace, along with those who call on the Lord out of a pure heart. 23 Don't have anything to do with foolish and stupid arguments, because you know they produce quarrels. 24 And the Lord's servant must not be quarrelsome but must be kind to everyone, able to teach, not resentful. 25 Opponents must be gently instructed, in the hope that God will grant them repentance leading them to a knowledge of the truth, 26 and that they will come to their senses and escape from the trap of the devil, who has taken them captive to do his will.

I like to refer to us as the radio, or tv station. That vessel that God or the devil works through to reach and teach others. Each of us have a choice with every single decision we make to work for God, or work for the devil. Once we discern this, things begin to change in our hearts, minds, and souls. Until now, you may have thought, " I am just defending myself", "God does not want anyone to hurt me." You may post on social media all the needs, wants, or struggles you have. You post thinking, " how will anyone know that I need help", or "how will they know what I am going through" if I do not share. Does any of this sound familiar? This is trusting in yourself, and others not God. If you truly believe that God is your protector, provider, healer, defender, the King of Kings, and the Lord of Lords then you would act like it.

    This does not happen overnight, especially if you just being informed now of how loudly your actions and reactions speak over your mouth! We first must realize that our weapons are not of the world, they are of divine power from God. Once we learn this, we can begin to identify the true enemy in a situation and use God's word to fight the good fight of faith.

    2 Corinthians 10:4 NIV ⁴ The weapons we fight with are not the weapons of the world. On the contrary, they have divine power to demolish strongholds.

    God knows that we have fallen for the tricks of the enemy. Now it feels odd or awkward to apply God's way, truth, and life to a situation when you have been taught to sass back, fight back, gossip, gather a cheer team, run to the hospital or cops. Those things bring temporary relief . They also cause more issues, if not with that person, for sure it causes a separation between you and God. Thank God, His mercy endures forever.

    This book was heavily prayed over that it would bring wisdom and understanding to the reader as well as transformation to your mind, mouth, and motives. With prayer this book will help you to saturate your heart, mind, and soul with the word of God. The word of God is the promises that God left behind on this earth for you and me. The word of God is the instruction manual that each of us came with at birth. When you open that new bike, or that playhouse. Do you toss the instructions. Do you look at the big picture on the box then try to put it together? You always end up with extra parts that way, right? Then your bike or playhouse is never fully equipped to work as it intended. The small details have been skipped and missed on purpose from lack of patience. Maybe your parent, or guardian tossed the instruction manual when you were given to them. Maybe no one gave them the instruction manual. Consider your parents were just handed the parts and was told, here put it together. Now you have the option to go back and get that instruction manual. It is yours and it is the Word of God. It is packed with instructions, examples, journals and love letters from God, it has all your promises and plans in there and it even has the best treasure map in it, that leads straight to heaven.

You cannot make it in this world without the weapons that God has given you. You can find these weapons in the word of God only. The Word of God teaches you how to use these weapons. The Word of God gives you all the armor you need to fight the good fight of faith.

Ephesians 6:10-18 NIV   The Armor of God [10] *Finally, be strong in the Lord and in his mighty power.* [11] *Put on the full armor of God, so that you can take your stand against the devil's schemes.* [12] *For* our struggle is not against flesh and blood, but against the rulers, against the authorities, against the powers of this dark world and against the spiritual forces of evil in the heavenly realms. ¹³ Therefore put on the full armor of God, so that when the day of evil comes, you may be able to stand your ground, and after you have done everything, to stand. ¹⁴ <u>Stand firm then, with the belt of truth buckled around your waist, with the breastplate of righteousness in place</u>. ¹⁵ and <u>with your feet fitted with the readiness that comes from the gospel of peace</u>. ¹⁶ In addition to all this, <u>take up the shield of faith</u>, with which you can extinguish all the flaming arrows of the evil one. ¹⁷ <u>Take the helmet of salvation</u> and <u>the sword of the Spirit</u>, which is the word of God. ¹⁸ And pray in the Spirit on all occasions with all kinds of prayers and requests. With this in mind, be alert and always keep on praying for all the Lord's people.

Armor up will show you truly how to put on the Armor of God. It will also teach you how to remember the Armor of God is on you. It will teach you how to access the weapons that God has given you. These weapons look like love, joy, peace, patience, kindness, goodness, faithfulness, gentleness, and self-control. Immediately your flesh may be saying, that sounds great but in a heated fight, major illness, or financial bind my mind is having trouble comprehending these beautiful words could fight such an ugly mess. That is because until now, you thought the only way to overcome is by using fear, worry, doubt, anger, pity, manipulation, control, gossip, and pride. Look back and tell me, did you ever truly win those battles or are you still in them?

This book is going to help you to see and know that the Lord is good and faithful. You will learn how to transform your mind, mouth, and motives to line up with God's word. This will not only change your actions and reactions. It will also break generational curses and bring forth generational blessings to the third and fourth generation. Know that one person's change, makes a huge difference. Look at Adam, look at Jesus! So now that you know this, let's learn how to show this!

CHAPTER 1

Buckle the Belt of Truth!

John 14:6 NIV *⁶Jesus answered, "I am the way and the truth and the life. No one comes to the Father except through me.*

Jesus is our truth! Let's learn how to put Jesus on around our waist. Let's learn your access of the truth in Christ Jesus, and how to apply that weapon. We are told that Jesus died for us to save us from our sin. We are told He was resurrected and is one with God in spirit and truth. We are told that we each have the Holy Spirit living inside of us once we are saved. Our mind knows this, but our mind has trouble activating this when we are in action, and especially in a reaction.

Once you identify your flesh and spirit are separate but one, then it is easier for you to learn home much more your spirit can and will do for you. Sure, we can line up our flesh with our spirit, or even drag our flesh along with us. However, if you constantly feeding your flesh and not your spirit then you will not have peace. Jesus teaches us we are what we eat. I love what Jesus says in Matthew 15: 16-18.

Matthew 15:16-18 NKJV **16** *So Jesus said, "Are you also still without understanding?* **17** *Do you not yet understand that whatever enters the mouth goes into the stomach and is eliminated?* **18** *But those things which proceed out of the mouth come from the heart, and they defile a man.*

Do you love how direct Jesus is? I love that about Him as well as His humor. I often hear this when I am in the middle of a "flesh moment" then softly hear " You Are What You Eat" Jill, do you want to be full of MESS or full of JESUS? Of course, we want to be full of Jesus. Of course, we want the prefect health and figure. However, when it comes to eating our vegetables and fruits, we often have a rough time choosing them over mac & cheese and cake, right?

The fruit we need to eat consist of the fruits of the spirit. These fruits look like love, joy, patience, kindness, goodness, faithfulness, gentleness, and self-control. However, we tend to want to eat things like hate, anger, anxiety, rudeness, fear, manipulation, and control. When you see the comparisons together, it may be clear which ones you want to have and want to receive from God. Putting that want into an action is the part we must activate with our belt of truth!

It is like saying I want to look like this model, then you decide to grab the ice cream because it looks delicious instead of the apple. I want big strong muscles, but you decide to play the latest game instead of workout. I want to get my bachelor's degree, then you get a job and settle instead of studying hard to get there. I will win that race, I am determined, but you never train for it. You see most of us self-sabotage. We want to be mad at the person with the degree, the model, the one with the great muscles, or the one that always seems to win the race. However, the truth is we do not want to put in the effort they did for it.

You also have people that study, show up, work hard, try their very best and never increase due to fear, worry, and lack of faith. You end up with all this information, and knowledge then never apply it to our life. You see this most often with Christians. They go to church time and time again. They study, they show up, they give, they love to gather. They learn the word through and through with the wisdom that God has, and God will do all things we ask. However, when a circumstance arises the first weapon the pull out is from the devil not God!

John 8:31-32 ESV The Truth Will Set You Free
31 So Jesus said to the Jews who had believed him, "If you abide in my word, you are truly my disciples, 32 and you will know the truth, and the truth will set you free."

Jill Deville

John 8:36 ESV ³⁶ *So if the Son sets you free, you will be free indeed.*

This means Jesus is our truth. The belt of truth! But you must show that you believe Jesus. Do not miss this in the scripture. Jesus also says those that abide. Meaning those that diligently seek Him. Jesus has promised us what He can and will do in His word. Jesus is not pushy or complicated, we are. Jesus will wait on you to Show What You Know. Jesus gives us the belt of truth. We must remember to put it on.

We tend to leave the belt of truth at home, in the car, in the closet. Then when we are in a bind and caught with our pants down, we want to run and grab the belt. Jesus said I gave you the equipment to keep your pants up. I gave you the belt to keep you from being exposed. Why do you choose to not put it on first to avoid the set back. Why go through the exposure, the stress, the embarrassment? We can put on what Jesus gave us when we are getting dressed for the day. You may have to literally pretend you putting on a belt to line your mind up with your spirit. Remember your spirit is willing but sometimes that old flesh is weak. God knows this. He is the one that told us this. He is not surprised that you ran out the door without your belt. He is running right behind you each day saying here it is, take it! But we think we do not need it. We think it will be okay. We think it takes away for the look we want.

ARMOR UP

John 1:14 ESV And the Word became flesh and dwelt among us, and we have seen his glory, glory as of the only Son from the Father, full of grace and truth.

Jesus is the way, the truth, and the life. We need Him. We also need to know Jesus and not just know of Him. To know Jesus is to know that the way is:

1. The way Jesus died for you to save your life and give you access to salvation. (See John 3:16)
2. The way Jesus came to the earth in the flesh. Jesus walked out all the things you and I go through. Jesus done this to show us how to apply God's word in each scenario. Jesus' way will help you to live. (See Matthew 1-28)
3. The way Jesus taught you in scripture and sermons His truth.

To begin to abide in Jesus and put on that belt of truth is to live in that truth. His word is truth. If you believe His word is true it will truly begin to show through, you. How? In your actions and reactions, Show What You Know. Your actions and reactions show what you believe and who you believe. This will make you more accountable. You will be saying Lord I trust you, or Lord, I do not believe you.

Say you have trouble with cussing. There is always that one person in your life that you would not dare cuss in front of. For me, it was my grandmother I would not dare try it. Somehow, someway in front of that person you can hold your tongue. Here is a thought. If you respect, love and honor Jesus. If you know He is with you always. If you have that belt of truth on, you will feel His presence. You will know He is there. You will not want to cuss. Sure, He would not reach out and pop your mouth, like she would. But it truly will change your mind, mouth and motives knowing He is present.

Learn the fruits of the spirit. The fruit of the spirit is how you activate the spirit filled weapons within you. Your access to freedom. If you have these fruits and if you are showing these fruits in your actions and reactions, then you will certainly reap them too.

Galatians 5:22-23 NLT [22] But the Holy Spirit produces this kind of fruit in our lives: love, joy, peace, patience, kindness, goodness, faithfulness, [23] gentleness, and self-control. There is no law against these things!

Do not miss who gives you these fruits! When you have the Holy Spirit in you. You will fight the spiritual attacks in your life, with the divine spirit in you. You may say well, this fight was with my friend, she betrayed me. This fight was with my spouse they cheated on me. This fight is with a bill I cannot pay. This fight is with a health report I cannot comprehend. Know that none of these fights are with flesh. Not even one!

Ephesians 6:12 NIV For our struggle is not against flesh and blood, but against the rulers, against the authorities, against the powers of this dark world and against the spiritual forces of evil in the heavenly realms.

The battle may come to us and look like the flesh, or something of the world. That is okay, we have decided to walk by faith and not by sight. Therefore, that means we will decern and decide that we must Show What We Know. We learned that Jesus is our protector, we must now show it. We have learned that Jesus is our healer, we must show it. We have learned Jesus is our savior, we must show it. We have learned in the Sunday pew every service that we have to walk by faith and not sight, we must show it. We have learned that the Lord is our Shepard we shall not want, we must show it. We have worshiped and asked God to take all of us and make us all of Him, now we must show it.

How? Activate the weapons God has given you from the Holy Spirit. When we realize that we have a duty to help the person that is attacking us because they are under the foothold of the devil. We learn that the battle is personal between us and the devil. God says do not worry about what others think or say. Focus on what He promises you and then do it.

Matthew 7:15-20 NKJV You Will Know Them by Their Fruits [15] *"Beware of false prophets, who come to you in sheep's clothing, but inwardly they are ravenous wolves.* [16] *You will know them by their fruits. Do men gather grapes from thornbushes or figs from thistles?* [17] *Even so, every good tree bears good fruit, but a bad tree bears bad fruit.* [18] *A good tree cannot bear bad fruit, nor can a bad tree bear good fruit.* [19] *Every tree that does not bear good fruit is cut down and thrown into the fire.* [20] *Therefore by their fruits you will know them.*

If we are walking around with the fruits of the devil such as fear, anger, lust, worry, doubt, lying, cheating, stealing, manipulating, gossiping. Then we are not bearing (producing) good fruit. God sees that we know His word and He also sees that we prefer the outcome of the devils' words and weapons.

Hebrews 11:6 NKJV [6] *But without faith it is impossible to please Him, for he who comes to God must believe that He is, and that He is a rewarder of those who diligently seek Him.*

Jesus knows and can relate to you in your stress, trauma, and drama. He went through it all in the flesh too. Jesus decided to apply the promises of God, and when He did Jesus got the outcome God promised Him. Are you truly wanting the way, the truth, and the life God has for you? Are do you prefer your way, truth, and life you have for you? Are you tried of fighting with your flesh? Are you tried of being the warrior for everyone. Are you ready to put on the belt of truth and understand, and know it is time to Show What You Know?

John 16:13 ESV When the Spirit of truth comes, he will guide you into all the truth, for he will not speak on his own authority, but whatever he hears he will speak, and he will declare to you the things that are to come.

Challenge : Be ready in truth. When you get dressed in the morning make it a habit to use your imagination and put on your belt of truth. (God teaches us in Matthew 18, unless we can come to Him like a child, we will never see the kingdom of Heaven) so toss the idea of this being silly and decide to do it.

Scripture: Learn this scripture. Write it on an index card, put it on your alarm label instead of "wake up" or "my alarm" .Decide to use your promise in memory and in prayer. This is your weapon.

ROMANS 9: 1 NIV I speak the truth in Christ—I am not lying, my conscience confirms it through the Holy Spirit—

Application: This is how you activate your belt, verse, and awareness that God is with you all day and all night. He promises us, even the ones that are forgetful that the Holy Spirit will remind you.

Prayer : Lord I will speak the truth in Christ, I am not lying, my conscience confirms it through the Holy Spirit in Jesus name amen.

Receive: Say Lord I will sow in the truth from my mouth, Lord I want to reap the truth from you and from others in Jesus's name amen.

If you take the step to pick up your armor of God, (the belt of truth) and apply the word of God in your life (your spiritual weapon) you will begin to reap truth (because you sowed that truth in). God's truth will be activated in your life, and it will show in your actions and reactions.

Learn there are many forms of a lying tongue such as exaggeration, half-truths, and white lies. There are many others as well. If it is not the full truth, then you are lying. That should help you to walk in truth.

Journal: Write down what you have gained from this chapter and how you can apply God's word (the belt of truth) in your life. Be bold and honest with yourself and write down the things you need help in with your flesh. The things you resorted to that got you by. This will help you as your transform to a new creation in Christ. When you look

ARMOR UP

back to these journal notes you will see your growth. You will also have a goal and feel more accountable to make that change, knowing that the things you show in your actions and reactions is truly what you believe in to be true.

_____

SAY IT: *1 Peter 1:13 ESV Therefore, preparing your minds for action, and being sober-minded, set your hope fully on the grace that will be brought to you at the revelation of Jesus Christ.*

PRAY IT: *Lord prepare my mind for action, make me sober-minded, set my hope fully on the grace that will be brought to me at the revelation of Jesus Christ in Jesus name amen.*

CHAPTER 2

Put on the Breastplate

2 Corinthians 5:20-21 NIV *²⁰ We are therefore Christ's ambassadors, as though God were making his appeal through us. We implore you on Christ's behalf: Be reconciled to God. ²¹ God made him who had no sin to be sin[a] for us, so that in him we might become the righteousness of God.*

I absolutely love these verses. Sit for a moment and just think about what these verses mean to you. Paul is sharing with us, that you are the billboards, the social platform, the representative of Jesus Christ! That is powerful! To put on your breastplate of righteousness could sound a little intimidating. For some, you may be thinking I am not worthy. You are wrong, you are. For others, you may be thinking, give it here, God can not do this without me. You are wrong, He can but He does not want to. For the faithful, you may be thinking I am going to put it on no matter what. I cannot do this without Him. You are right, you cannot. You do not have to do anything alone. Jesus just calls us to seek Him first and His righteousness, then all will be added to us. Do not miss the "and" in that verse.

Matthew 6:33 NKJV ³³ But seek first the kingdom of God and His righteousness, and all these things shall be added to you.

    Decide to get up and put the breastplate of righteousness on. Do this with a love and desire to want to be as close to God as possible. Knowing if you put on His armor, you will feel that presence of Him in and around you. Let that be enough. Again, you may have to physically pretend to put on the breastplate. This will help your mind line up with your belief in Jesus Christ and His promises to you. Righteousness means to be in right standing with Christ. Again, you may be thinking how in this world could I be in right standing with Jesus. He does everything right; I tend to have trouble getting out of bed without an attitude in the morning. How could I go all day without sin? The answer is you cannot. His word says so. That is why you need Him, and that is why He died for you.

    He did not die for you to habitually sin with reasoning, and carefree. He died for you so that His blood would cover a multitude of sin with His mercy, and grace. What is the difference? Isn't sin, a sin? Yes, it is. However, if you know you doing wrong, and you do not desire to change that wrong, there are consequences for that sin. You will reap from that sin into your life and to the life of your generation.

James 1: 13- 15 13 When tempted, no one should say, "God is tempting me." For God cannot be tempted by evil, nor does he tempt anyone; 14 but each person is tempted when they are dragged away by <u>their own evil desire and enticed</u>. 15 Then, after desire has conceived, it gives birth to sin; and sin, when it is full-grown, gives birth to death.

Your spiritual weapon is wisdom, knowing you cannot put the action or reaction on the enemy. Your heart, your belief system has just been revealed. Whatever you do in action and reaction is activated directly from your heart and now is coming out of your mind, mouth, and motives. It shows what and who you believe. God or the devil. Your action and reaction reveal who you trust in. God or the devil. Your action and reaction reveal what weapon you just picked up. Was it one from God or the devil? Your spirit filled weapon should be a weapon from God because you have already put on your breastplate. You put on that breastplate so that your mind would comprehend you are already protected by God. You do not have to worry about any weapons penetrating through to harm you. Therefore, you can be confident using God's weapons for the battle.

This may be easy to say, maybe even great to know. But how do you truly apply this when someone is coming at you to hurt you?

ARMOR UP

As you begin to learn what Jesus done throughout the bible. You will learn He endured it all for you. We needed that example of how to be Christ Like. How to be that billboard, that ambassador for Christ. Let me encourage you to read the book of Matthew. From chapter 1 to 28 you will learn about the life of Jesus. The way, the truth, the life.

You will see what Jesus done when He was tested by the devil in Matthew 4. You will see what Jesus done when He was approached by people that were in sin. He taught them in an action with love. He did not hate them, he hated the sin. He showed us to use the evidence of the sin on someone as a billboard for our mission. He took it as an invite to rescue them from their battle. While the devil was trying to convince Him, that he had a battle. Jesus did not fall for it. Jesus wants us to no longer fall for it either.

Jesus teaches us in the word of God that this person that appears to be our enemy is a victim of sin, and the devil. They need you to intercede for them. Our normal is to feel attacked, betrayed, hurt, pitiful, or prideful. Know that this is both schemes from the devil and weapons of the world. You may choose to use those weapons of the world. Maybe the devil convinced you that they work the best. I want to ask you, have they really worked? Are you still in that battle?

Jesus showed us that the elders, the church, the law, the people, and the kings came against Him too. When they did, He stood firm with the weapons of divine power. You see, their weapons were not working. Their weapons look like murder, anger, addiction, greed, lust, worry, control, and religion. His weapons look like love, joy, peace, patience, kindness, goodness, faithfulness, and self-control. One was weapons of the world; one was weapons of divine power. Which weapons do you tend to pick up? Christians that have put on the breastplate of righteousness will show this in their actions and reactions. They will learn that having the breastplate on the floor or in the closet will not help them. Having it, is never enough. You must use it.

James 1:21-22 NKJV Doers—Not Hearers Only
[21] Therefore lay aside all filthiness and [a] overflow of wickedness, and receive with <u>meekness the implanted word, which is able to save your souls.</u> [22] But be doers of the word, and not hearers only, deceiving yourselves.

Jesus teaches us that He is our protector, healer, provider, and Savoir. When we train our brain to put on His protection and use His weapons, then things change. Jesus teaches and protects us with simplicity because He wanted everyone to understand and have no excuse. He even came down in the flesh to walk it out for us by example so that we could not say, "Jesus you do not understand." Jesus understands every day. Jesus knows what it's like to be rejected, avoided, mistreated, and hated. The sad part is He feels this from us. The enemy does not always look like the enemy. Most of the time, it looks like a beautiful Christian that lacks faith, wisdom, and understanding. Something that seems to be so laid out and simple, tends to be so hard. Why is that? Because we prefer to please the world, which consist of us and others. We are used to making excuses or justifications and getting away with it or getting by.

    Jesus wants us to know He did not die on the battlefield of this world for us to not have freedom. The word specially says for the Son set us free, so we are free indeed (John 8:36). Jesus lived in the flesh to feel what we feel and to fight what we fight. The difference is He fights for us because He loves us so much. We need to love Him so much that we would be willing to sacrifice just the filth from our life. He is not asking for us to give up the good stuff, like He had to. He is asking for you just to hand Him the bad stuff. He wants you to let Him fight the battle for you. He is your divine power. He is embedded in your breastplate. He is just asking you to take it out of the closet and put it on.

    Be like Christ, be that ambassador. Decide to walk in right standing with Christ. Jesus was approached with people infected by the devil's schemes. Those people did not look like the devil, those people were not devil worshipers. Those people looked and was convinced they were a murderer, ill, disabled, mean, greedy, whores, thieves. Jesus showed us that if you look pass the scheme of the enemy. You will see the mission from God. Jesus teaches you that as you learn the word of God (your weapon), you will learn wisdom, understanding, courage and discernment.

Think about this. You just learned to love your enemy while reading the word of God or in a Sunday service. Then here that enemy comes. Maybe the first thing you want to do is retreat in fear or attack in furry. Stop for a second and mediate on why this enemy was able to approach you at all. Especially, if you just learned about how to address, fight, and act with an enemy. Are you being tested like Job? He was a faithful man of God. He loved the Lord. He was a wealthy man and yet He kept his focus and trust in God. But when the devil spoke to God, he said Job only loves you because he has it all. So, God said, take everything but his life. My child is not going to waver. He knows my word, he knows my promises, and he knows I am right here. How will you show what you know, if you are never truly approached to activate that truth? You can be a great Christian all alone, or when things go your way. But when it is time to apply what you know, do you know the word at all. Most importantly do you believe within your heart and apply it?

I can be the best Christian until my teen gets home. Then I want to pull out a "world weapon" and argue back. Are do I pull out the " spirit filled weapon" and pray and correct. I can decide to walk off . I can decide to pray for me and her to not have a spirit of fear but of love, power, and sound mind. I can ask God to give us both ears to hear and eyes to see. Arguing back elevates the enemy and causes a division for a moment or more. Praying and seeking God rebukes the schemes of the enemy, reveals the true reason they want to argue and brings you closer to each other and God.

ARMOR UP

    I will give you an example. I picked up my daughter and she had an attitude. I was having a great day. Now I choose to be irritated. My mind goes to " I just left work to pick up this ungrateful sassy child". My motives go to argue with her the entire way back to work. Then of course I am going to post about it. Then I will have an attitude with others because of it. I will then be miserable the rest of the day. I am going to share how mad I am with my spouse. Now he is going to be frustrated. Does this Sound familiar? Do you see the plague?? Hate spreads like a plague. It is the enemy's scheme. The devil does not care if it is in the form of covid or hate. All he cares about is that he is infecting and killing people with something simple or huge. We have the choice to pick up the weapon from him, or we have the choice to pick up the weapon from God. God's weapons work best and look like this. Would you like to pray about whatever is bothering you? NO! Would you like to talk about it? NO! JUST LEAVE ME ALONE! Ok, but know I will pray for you. You will not disrespect me. I did not hurt you. I am sorry someone else hurt you, I am here when you are ready to talk. Be bold and say, God taught us how to fight our battles and this is not how.

    I know what you are thinking, this is not going to work, and this is off some sort of sitcom. I am going to punish this brat because she is being disrespectful. I do not have to tolerate it. I know because I was there before. I would have tossed this book with that very statement. Why? Because I had not seen the divine power of Jesus. I did not know how His weapons worked. Those weapons seemed weak and powerless to me. I did not know about them (as a Christian) nor would I know how to use them if I had. God teaches faith without works is dead in James 2. If we read this, and if we know this. Then we must show this in these things. That is our weapon.

The devil wants you convinced that you are weak. That this is stupid. That they will run all over you. Jesus teaches you in His way, truth, and life that His weapons are powerful and life changing. Your mind begins to transform with the power and authority of Jesus. He gives you wisdom and understanding. That wisdom and understanding brings peace, love, and joy into your heart, mind, and soul. Yes, you can punish them. Yes, you can whip them if that is what you promised when they done wrong. But you must also do those things with love. If they are not with love, then you are wrong too. You begin to see the enemy even if it is a horrible person or your child as the weak one. The one that needs you. You begin to see things like Jesus because you become reconciled with Him.

Ephesians 6:11-15 NIV ¹¹ Put on the full armor of God, so that you can take your stand against the devil's schemes. ¹² For our struggle is not against flesh and blood, but against the rulers, against the authorities, against the powers of this dark world and against the spiritual forces of evil in the heavenly realms. ¹³ Therefore put on the full armor of God, so that when the day of evil comes, you may be able to stand your ground, and after you have done everything, to

ARMOR UP

stand. ¹⁴ Stand firm then, with the belt of truth buckled around your waist, with the <u>breastplate of righteousness in place</u>, ¹⁵ and with your feet fitted with the readiness that comes from the gospel of peace.

    As for me, I know that the weapons I used that were influenced by the devil for decades did not win any battles. They may have had me feel like I won at times, but I truly never did. The armor I used from the devil was more like walls. They left me feeling prideful or pitiful. The weapons I used were more like stones. They left me feeling controlling or fearful. They never had me feel like a warrior.

    Therefore, if you can be the best Christian until the air conditioner breaks. Then you want to pull out a "world weapon" and complain, and resort to anger or pride saying things like "I do not deserve this" or "I work hard why do I have to be in a hot house." You need to ask why, and where does this come from. God says the things that come out of our mouth come from our hearts. Those weapons from the devil will not work. They do not resolve the issue. They do not win the battle.

    God teaches us to do what we know to do, while He does the rest. Do not be deceived by the devil. Put your hands on that air conditioner and say, Lord am I taking care of this properly, or does it just need maintenance? If it needs maintenance please provide the funds, and the favor to get this repaired timely. Lord if I need to take care of this better then give me wisdom on when and how. Give me the courage to make the time and do it. Lord if the enemy is messing with my air condition, I rebuke him and demand he leave now in the name of Jesus. Yes, I do it. No, it is not stupid. It is divine power. Try it. It works! If you can use the weapons of the world and complain for days or decades. You can take a minute and say something powerful in the spirit and see it happen. Claiming what is bad, surely has been working for you. Therefore, be like our brother Joseph in Genesis 50:19-20 and use it for your good and the good of many others. Speak like, speak the promises of God over it. God teaches us the power is in our tongue.

Genesis 50:19-20 NIV [19] But Joseph said to them, "Don't be afraid. Am I in the place of God? [20] You intended to harm me, but God intended it for good to accomplish what is now being done, the saving of many lives.

Joseph did not use all the horrible things people did to him as an excuse to do evil. Joseph decided to apply the word of God and remain faithful to God. Joseph discerned how to use divine weapons. Take the time to study about Joseph (Genesis 37-50) let that be your next book you read or stop now and come back another time. You will learn how to use your armor and weapons from God and how grand the outcome is when you decide to Show What You Know.

ARMOR UP

Proverbs 18:20-21 NIV ²⁰ *From the <u>fruit of their mouth</u> a <u>person's stomach is filled</u>; with the <u>harvest of their lips</u> they are satisfied.* ²¹ *The <u>tongue has the power of life and death</u>, and those who love it will eat its fruit.*

It comes back to the fruit. Jesus wants us to be reminded if you are of Him, you will show it. Jesus reminds us, if you are filling up on His word, then His word will come out of your actions and reactions. This is important because we need others to know we are Christians by our actions and reactions. Not our t-shirts, jewelry, or titles. You would be insulted if you purchased a box of brownies and got home and broccoli was in the box, right? If our labels do not match the ingredients inside the box, then that is not going to work. We are made in the image of God to be ambassadors for Christ. That means people need to know Christ lives in us. His fruits are in our basket. Let those fruits look so grand, that others take from that basket and eat to be filled with God too. You are meant to be the advertisement for Jesus. Therefore, decide today to Show What You Know.

Challenge : Be ready in right standing (righteousness). When you get dressed in the morning make it a habit to use your imagination. Put on your breastplate of righteousness with your belt of truth. This will help you to be aware of the armor you have on you. This will help you to understand nothing can harm you. See Exodus

14:14.

Scripture: Learn this scripture. Write it down several times, put it where you will brush your teeth and repeat until you know it. Decide to use your promise in memory and in prayer. This is your weapon.

Exodus 14:14 NIV **¹⁴** *The LORD will fight for you; you need only to be still."*

Application: This is how you activate your breastplate, verse, and awareness that God is with you all day and all night and will fight for you.

Prayer : Lord I know that you will fight for me, I need only to be still in Jesus' name amen.

Receive: Say Lord I will receive this promise. I am deciding to speak life from my mouth because life (Jesus) is in me.

If you take the step to pick up your armor of God, (the breastplate of righteousness) and apply the word of God in your life (your spiritual weapon) you will begin believing and show it in your actions and reactions in your life. Because you are showing what you believe. Remember God breathed life into you. Now it is time that you breathe life into others. They can get to know Jesus because you introduce them to Him in your behavior.

Journal: Write down who you tend to speak bad of. Maybe it is you, maybe someone that has hurt you, or maybe a loved one. Only you know. To help you gather your thoughts, it sounds like this:
1. Why do they wear or do this.
2. I do not know why they are so horrible.
3. They are such a liar.
4. They steal from everyone.
5. I will always hurt.
6. They will never stop using.
7. Everyone does not like me.
8. They are lazy, prideful, selfish, fat, skinny, whatever!
9. I will never get to do that because I am a mom, child, teen, stupid, lazy, busy, etc.

Decide to speak life. Decide you were just chosen to be that person's prayer warrior. Think about it. If it bothers your flesh and stirs up your spirit it is for a purpose. If you are of God, then decide you have been invited to intercede because God trust you with this person. Let that be the reason you feel some sort of way, let it be to pray.

SAY IT: *Psalms 51:10 Create in me a pure heart, O God, and renew a steadfast spirit within me.*

PRAY IT: *Lord Create in me a pure heart, O God and renew a steadfast spirit within me in Jesus' name amen.*

ARMOR UP

CHAPTER 3

Fit your Feet in Peace

Romans 13: 11- 14 NIV 11 Besides this you know the time, that the hour has come for you to wake from sleep. For salvation is nearer to us now than when we first believed. 12 The night is far gone; the day is at hand. So then let us cast off the works of darkness and put on the armor of light. 13 Let us walk properly as in the daytime, not in orgies and drunkenness, not in sexual immorality and sensuality, not in quarreling and jealousy. 14 But put on the Lord Jesus Christ, and make no provision for the flesh, to gratify its desires.

What a powerful and bold set of scriptures. Jesus wants us to know the time has come to decide will you walk in the spirit or the flesh. Ask yourself do I tend to walk in the spirit or the flesh more? Do others know that I have a relationship with Jesus, or do they not know at all? Do you tend to like the things done in the darkness (sin)? Are do you try to walk upright in the light (showing that you are saved)? Once you know these scriptures it is hard to lie to yourself or others any longer. It is hard to make excuses without feeling convicted by God. I can hear Him each time say, "Really Jill" . Then I resort to say, No Sir, I should not have said or done that. At first, it did not go that way. I would make a ton of excuses, like they should not have done that. If I do not say anything they will hurt me again or others. If I do not speak up or post about it how will others be protected. I would go but I have work , I am busy or tired. But when the "Really Jill" got louder I could no longer ignore it. Then eventually I no longer wanted to ignore it. Learning integrity and honesty will show your growth in your choices. It will show your growth with Jesus. It helps us to decide to walk with your armor on your feet, or to toss it and get defeated ? I heard a joke once; it went something like this. You know why God chose the snake to represent the devil? Because he is de-feeted! Ha! (He has no feet) You see his outcome is already represented in his appearance. Also, if you look at the very last chapter of the Bible, God wins. The devil is always meant to be defeated.

If God wins and you are of God, then guess what? You win too. We need to stop being tricked by the enemy and learn to walk by faith and not by site. I know what you are thinking. The site of my bills, health, house, parents, spouse, grades, job, circumstance are clear. However, when we decide to look at things with the promises of God, that is your divine power. That is your weapon. We tend to believe the enemies traps over God's provision. Before you say no. What does your actions say? It is in our reaction to the situation that reveals who we trust in. This reaction comes from our heart. Exposing this is a grand thing. Do not let it discourage you. Let it encourage you. Now we can line up our flesh with our spirit. We know that God is and God has the power. But somehow our mind and body do not want to cooperate with our "knower" (soul), right? In this book we will learn how to align our mind and body to follow Jesus. We will learn how to fix our eyes and our feet on Jesus.

2 Corinthians 5:7 NKJV ⁷For we walk by faith, not by sight.

Can we agree this is a short and easy scripture to learn. Most of us have heard it before. Most of us believe it but we do not show it. Let's decide to challenge ourselves today to memorize this verse. Stop and write it down and put it in your phone. Maybe add it to your calendar for the entire month. That way this will be the first thing you pull up or see when you begin your day. Once you memorize it, you will hear it more in your day to day lives. You will be more aware of it in your actions and reactions, and you will use it. When the Holy Spirit reminds you of this verse you will hear it now because it will be familiar to your mind and body. This will allow your mind and body to press into this promise (this weapon) so that you can fight with divine power.

Knowing your promises and having your weapons and not using them; is like watching a video on exercising and expecting to lose weight. You see the exercise. You know about the exercise. You see the people on the video toned more and more each week. But you never put down the ice cream and do the exercise. OUCH!

Thank God this is not a book about losing weight or exercising, right? This is about losing sin! This is about losing stress. This is about you no longer losing the battle because you now will use divine power to fight.

Knowing about the word of God. Seeing the word of God. Hearing the word of God is not enough. Knowing about Jesus. Knowing what Jesus done for you is not enough. You need to know Jesus, not just know of Jesus. God literally came down to earth in the flesh for you and me as Jesus to live in the flesh. Why? To relate to us. To show us how to walk in the way, the truth, and the life. To be a light to our path. To help us put on our armored boots.

John 1: 1- 5 NKJV *[1] In the beginning was the Word, and the Word was with God, and the Word was God. [2] He was with God in the beginning. [3] Through him all things were made; without him nothing was made that has been made. [4] In him was life, and that life was the light of all mankind. [5] The light shines in the darkness, and the darkness has not overcome[a] it.*

There is nothing that can overcome Jesus. We just must learn to run to Him and activate Him. Then we will start to win these battles we face in our everyday lives. These battles are not with flesh and blood. These battles are with spirits therefore if we truly use spiritual warfare we will win. We learned in the prior chapters that we were called to be that prayer warrior for that person, place or thing that comes against us. They are the victim of the devil and sin. Knowing the word of God, and that Jesus resides in us will give us wisdom and understanding. Wisdom and understanding gives us strength to walk in His way, truth, and life. That typically never looks like the way we were taught in tradition or religion. Having a relationship with Christ and knowing His word gives us a divine weapon. Both give us a choice to win if we decide to do what Jesus would do.

So how do you use spiritual warfare? We use God's promises. We put on God's armor. This will help us to walk with confidence, courage, and strength. This will manifest the fruits of the spirit within us. Our action of God's word will be evidence that you know you have the armor of God on. It will look like peace and self- control. In this chapter you will learn how to put on the armored boots. This will help your mind to align with your faith and walk in God's truth. Not the truth of the enemy.

John 10:10 NKJV *¹⁰ The thief does not come except to steal, and to kill, and to destroy. I have come that they may have life, and that they may have it more abundantly.*

When we recognize it was not the mother, the spouse, the friend, or the brother that just attacked us, rejected us, hurt us, or betrayed us. We will begin to know how to fight back and win. The war is spiritual. God gives us the armor and the weapons. To be clear, those weapons are His word of God. It has all the examples we need. Then God teaches us how to put on the armor with child like faith knowing God is our protector. Once we know His word and once, we have literally put on His armor we will act like it. We will walk with assurance and courage. You will notice you feel more confident.

Jesus teaches us He is the way, the truth, and the life. If you walk in His way, truth, and life with your boots you will have peace. You will have the divine power to demolish strongholds and have the peace above all understanding Jesus speaks of.

Ephesians 6:15 NKJV [15] *and with your feet fitted with the readiness that comes from the gospel of peace.*

How do you put on these boots. When you put on your socks, shoes, lotion. Say Lord I am putting on my armored boots so that I can walk in peace. Doesn't that seem so simple. Doesn't that seem a little silly. That is what the devil wants you to feel, silly and simple. All this time you could have stopped so many attacks, worry and fear with one simple action. The only set back is someone did not share it with you, or you did not want to do it because it seems simple or silly. The devil kills, steals, and destroys. If he can make you feel ridiculous, he will. But Jesus says I came to give you life in abundance, but you must have child-like faith.

When I was reading in Matthew 18 for the first time. I was in awe of Jesus. The disciples had been walking with Him day and night. They had left their homes, their jobs, their families and decided to walk and follow Jesus. They had come to a crowd and the children were trying to see and talk with Jesus. The adults were trying to tell them not to bother Jesus. Then Jesus picked up one of the children and told the disciples unless you can follow me like a child, then you will not enter the kingdom of Heaven.

I could just picture their faces and body language again right now. They had to feel like, all the "work" and "sacrifice" was for nothing. Jesus was not trying to discredit none of that. He was ensuring them that being with Him was not enough. Seeing what He could do and did do was not enough. They needed to be like Him. Jesus teaches us faith without works is dead. He also teaches us we can not earn His salvation. What does this mean? It means your belief needs to be an action. You need to literally turn to Him in your life and with your life. You must ask for forgiveness for your sins to begin this relationship with Jesus. Then you must ask for forgiveness each time you sin thereafter. Repentance does not just mean asking for forgiveness and acknowledging Jesus died and rose for you. It also means turning to Jesus. Turning to Him looks like diligently seeking Him and His way, truth, and life. Turning away from Him looks like believing the facts, and the world over the promises that Jesus gives us. Turning away from Jesus looks like doing things that Jesus would not do. Turning away from Jesus looks like pleasing the world and yourself instead of Jesus.

The things that he has to offer you has been stolen from you by the devil. The devil has made you believe for far to long that you have to fit in, fight for yourself, provide for yourself, and run to lust instead of love. The devil has made you feel that if you reveal you are of God that you will seem weak and stupid. The devil has made you believe that the weapons of the world can help you more than the weapons of divine power. He has made you believe that worrying, complaining, doubting, fearing, cussing, gossiping, slandering, stealing, lying, cheating, manipulating is greater, and more powerful for you. He has made those things your way, truth, and life. You show that these weapons mean more to you in your actions and reactions to your battles.

Jesus wants us to use our weapons of divine power. Those weapons should reflect the fruits of the spirit which is powered by faith. Faith is growing in peace, patience, love, joy, faithfulness, kindness, goodness, gentleness, and self-control. You see, that thought right there. How in the world could I have that? How in the world can I use this as a weapon? Because you are deciding today that it worked for Jesus, so it can work for you. Today you are learning that it is not silly or simple at all to have these weapons. These weapons are hard to figure out. These weapons are hard to access. These weapons are hard to even pull out and use. But they are the best and most productive weapons because they are of divine power. They can win any battle because they are spirit filled with faith in action.

We seem to be the best Christian until work slows down. We seem to be the best Christian until we get sick or a bad health report. We seem to be the best Christian until we see others on vacation, and we are stuck at home or work broke. We seem to be the best Christian until someone does not want to help us. We seem to be the best Christian until someone does not answer our call or text back. Paul teaches us in Philippians 4:13 that we can do all things through Christ Jesus that strengthens us. But when we cannot do something, we wonder why Jesus is not helping us. It is because you did not realize verse 10-12 was your promise too.

You see Paul teaches he learned how to be consent well feed or hungry. He learned to be content broke or rich. He learned to be content with friends or without. He also learned how to be content with help or without. Then he goes on to say I can do all things through Christ Jesus who strengthens me. This means he was only able to have that peace and self-control above all understanding because his understanding and faith was in Jesus Christ. We must learn how to walk like Paul did in the path that Jesus showed us. You can see the life of Jesus in the book of Matthew from Chapter one to twenty-eight.

Know that you can not walk like Jesus unless you read His word and understand the armored boots He wore. His boots you never saw them, but you knew they were there. You knew they were their because Jesus walked by faith and not by sight. Those armored boots are being shared with you in this chapter. They will allow you to start walking by faith and not by sight. They will give you a new confidence. They will give you courage. You will know and comprehend you have them on. Therefore, even when the facts are loud and clear you will know that His facts are loud and clear too. You will be reminded by the Holy Spirit that God wins all battles. You will learn from the Holy Spirit that you win if you put on His boots.

Challenge : Decide to put on the armored boots given to you. When you are putting on your shoes, socks, or even your lotion say I am putting your armored boots on Lord. Help me to walk in your way, your truth, and your life. I receive the peace that comes with these boots in Jesus name amen.

Scripture: Learn this scripture. Write it down several times, put it where you will brush your teeth and repeat until you know it. Decide to use your promise in memory and in prayer. This is your weapon.

2 Corinthians 5:7 NKJV 7 For we walk by faith, not by sight.

Application: This is how you activate your boots, verse, and

ARMOR UP

awareness that God is with you all day and all night and will fight for you.

Prayer : Lord I will walk by faith and not by site in Jesus name amen.

Receive: Say Lord I receive your promises, I receive your provision, I receive your protection, I receive your healing, and thank you Lord that I do not have to walk alone in Jesus name amen.

Decide to speak life. Decide that no matter how the facts of the world or the circumstance looks you will trust in the Lord. Write down things you have trouble trusting the Lord with. Ask Him to help you in these things and to give you wisdom, understanding and healing in and for these things. Then each day write down how you applied His word instead of fear when these things came up. You will begin to see your growth. You will have something to look back to one day when you are going through other things. You will be your own Hope, knowing God won then and He will win again.

SAY IT: *Philippians 4:13 13 I can do all things through Christ who strengthens me.*

PRAY IT: *Lord I can do all things through Christ Jesus that strengthens me in Jesus name amen.*

CHAPTER 4

Take up the Sheild of Faith

Hebrews 11:1-3 NIV Faith in Action 11 Now faith is confidence in what we hope for and assurance about what we do not see. ² This is what the ancients were commended for. ³ By faith we understand that the universe was formed at God's command, so that what is seen was not made out of what was visible.

I love this verse it plainly tells us what faith is. Faith is the things you hope for that you know are true and look forward to. Faith is knowing God is over all. Knowing that no one can do more than God. There was no one, or nothing before God. Some may say, okay I believe this but let me encourage you today to see if you truly believe this. God's word teaches us that even the demons believe, and tremble and we know they are not going to heaven. Belief is an action word. It is not just a word to toss around.

You may flip the light switch on in your home knowing the lights will come on. You do this because you believed the lights will come on. You believe in electricity. You cannot see the electricity, but you do believe in it because you show it in an action. You may believe a chair will hold you when you sit on it. You believe it with your mind then you just sit on it. You do not check the legs, the weight restrictions or under it to see if anything is broken. You just sit, right? You leave your home; you get in your car, and you start the car. You do this because you know and believe it will start. You may call a parent for money to assist you. They will tell you sure come by it will be under the porch in the BBQ pit next to the door. You go to their home, and you go get it. That is because you have faith it will be there. It takes an action to show you believe. God wants this same belief. He wants you to have faith in Him.

Hebrews 11:6 NIV 6 And without faith it is impossible to please God, because anyone who comes to him must believe that he exists and that he rewards those who earnestly seek him.

Many teach and believe once saved always saved, and the bible does not teach that. To not linger here, or cause confusion let's get right to the point. I will remind you of the devil himself. He was a gorgeous angel. One over worship in heaven. He decided he would not follow God. He decided to choose pride and act as though he knew more than God. The devil thought he could do better than God. Then God sent him to hell. Just saying this convicted me, so I hope it convicted you too.

    We often get caught up in pride. You may think, not me. I am shy, I am weak, I know I mess up. I know I need God. Pride does not just look like a man beating on his chest saying I am the best and no one is better than me. Pride is not being proud of yourself for doing great things. Pride is when you get in front of God. Pride is when you put other things in front of God. Ouch! Pride is when you say, I will help this person out of jail for the ninth time. I will not even consider asking God what He wants me to do. I will not even consider God is putting them there to clean them out, to separate them from their temptations, or to protect them from death. You may want to be their God because you are prideful and not faithful. You may genuinely not even know this about yourself. You may even think you are doing what God has called you to do sincerely.

    But most of the time when it is a consistent issue with someone or yourself you are saying I can fix this God. I got this God. It is too big for you God. Now you may never say that, but your actions show that. Your actions show you have faith in you. Allot of times people are taught so poorly about the way, the truth, and the life (JESUS). They honestly think they are helping a person or Jesus by stepping in and giving, providing, and helping. They do not even consider that they are prideful and enabling. How do you know when to help and when not to? Most of us know we are helping because we want the glory, the thanks, the seed sown. That is just the truth. We need that truth out in the open. For the son sets us free so we are free indeed (John 8:36). But then there are the ones with the gift of giving. They have the time, the money, the faith, and they are just eager to help. They honestly do not want any attention for it. They want God to have all the glory. This still does not mean it is okay to always help. God wants us to seek Him first in all things, one of those gifts He gives us is also common sense, or as God calls it common use.

Romans 9:21 NIV Does not the potter have the right to make out of the same lump of clay some pottery for special purposes and some for common use?

Meaning deep down in your conscious you know if you should or should not help. You know if you should go bail someone out of their financial matter, or circumstance. You will know if you are helping them or hurting them. You will know if you are being manipulated to help or feel lead to help. God gives us that gift to know. Another way to check your "knower" (intentions) is when you help others are you expecting something in return from them, or even from God. God promises us in Matthew 6 when we help, fast, give, serve, and pray to do it with a cheerful heart in secret He will see us, and He will bless us how He sees fit. God also tells us if we do things in the open or expecting something in return that is all the reward we will get. The reward will come with limitations of your expectations on others or yourself. Wouldn't you rather use the weapon you have that teaches you to give, to help, to listen, to serve to transform you to your new natural way. The way of Jesus. That is your weapon of divine power. That is how you become that ambassador of Christ.

When you begin to use that weapon to give, listen, wait, serve you will begin to see battles won in all areas of your life. Strive to be like Jabez and Solomon. Their prayers were so mighty that Jesus blessed them abundantly because their prayers were not selfish. They asked to help others. They prayed more for others than for themselves. They trusted and focused on the Father and His business. They asked for wisdom and understanding on how they could serve Him and others. God saw their hearts and blessed them in every area of their lives spiritually, mentally, financially, and otherwise.

God is looking to see if we take the lead, or we follow His lead. God also teaches us faith without works is dead. We cannot just say we believe and then sit back and say Lord I got this. It is too big for you. Again, you may never dare say this especially to God. But does your actions show this.

We cannot be saved and think we can go about our day sinning habitually. Jesus knows we will sin and feel convicted and want change. Conviction is when we are embarrassed of our sins and humbly ask God to forgive us. We must be careful not to sin then say, well I had to. They would think they could run over me if I did not say or do this. Maybe you say things like I could not pay my bills because I needed this outfit and I deserve it. These things are pride too. These things are lack of faith. Never say give me what I deserve Lord because you surely will not like it.

Ephesians 2:8-9 NIV 8 For it is by grace you have been saved, through faith—and this is not from yourselves, it is the gift of God—9 not by works, so that no one can boast.

You see faith is showing you believe in God, you believe there is a God, and that God can and will do more than you or anyone else. Faith is knowing God's word and showing that you know it. Faith is applying God's word in your actions and reactions. Your actions and reactions show your true heart. Your heart shows what you hope in and who you believe. God is the Creator. If you believe in the creation so much, how much more can the Creator do for you. He is the one that created all the things you trust in. I pray seeing this from this point of view helps you to seek God first and His right standing so that all can be added to you. (Matthew 6:33) teaches us if we do seek God first, there is nothing we have limitations from. We are the stall by seeking ourselves or others first because we have faith in them. Let's decide to use our divine weapon of faith. Let's decide to hold that shield of faith up high.

Ephesians 6:16 In addition to all this, take up the shield of faith, with which you can extinguish all the flaming arrows of the evil one.

You see with faith we can fight the stress, worry, and fear. We have the armor. We just choosing not to use it. God gave us the shield of faith. Have you had a circumstance lately that seems to just defeat you. Maybe you have the strongest faith with your health. No matter

ARMOR UP

what, you know and show that you believe God can heal you. Maybe you have the strongest faith in God over your marriage. No matter what you know to go to God and He helps you through any circumstance in your marriage. This furoates the devil so then he tries to get to you with your children. Maybe they are just sassy. Maybe they are disrespectful. Maybe they are selfish. For some maybe you are dealing with them having an issue with money, health, addictions, or relationships. Maybe it is rejection. Somehow with all the faith you have and know with everything else we still tend to fall in that one spot. I call it that sucker punch right in the gut from the devil. Because he is desperate. The devil knows if he can distract you, then he can distract many that look up to you.

With these children some of us are like Job. Praying and fasting for them just in case they sin. Some know their children is in sin, and you just get so upset and worried that you become stressed or even sick. You see the enemy does not care if he distracts you with something large or small. He just wants you distracted. He wants you to call bad things out on your children. He wants you do feel defeated and like you have no faith. As a Christian we learn that the power is in our tongue. When we speak life, good things happen. When we speak death, bad things happen. This is because we are filled with the same power that rose Jesus from the grave.

I will give you an example. Let's say you battling with a selfish child. When someone ask you about this child. You smirk with your "holy self" and say they are selfish. I do not know what do to or say about them. You say this every time they do something selfish. You say this every time someone ask. So then ask yourself since you are the "Holy One" (the Christian) and they are not. Are you the reason they are still selfish? Ouch! You see Jesus is very direct with us in His word. He wants us to know the truth so that the truth will set us free. He wants us to live without excuse. He wants us to say, I done that because I wanted to. I done that because I was tempted. Please forgive me. He does not want us to say, I done this because they done this. Our children have free will. We can teach them the way they should go, as the Lord instructed us. Then they still may do whatever they want to do. However, we are still accountable to do what God teaches us to do in it. You are to show what you know. He often allows things to happen to see if we will show our belief with an action. He always prepares us before the battle. We just have to decide to pick up His weapons and put on His armor. This looks like faith. Or we have the chance to pick up the devil's armor and weapons. That looks like wrath, hate, pity which all equal defeat and fear.

  See the story of Job. No matter what, Job kept His faith. When Job kept his faith, God blessed Job abundantly. He gave him all he lost in abundance. You may read the book of Job and say, my gosh. you cannot just replace the children that died like the cattle, the money, or the house. You are right, you cannot. However, God knew those children. As you read the book of Job, you will see that they were having parties instead of time with God. They were replacing their time with God for these events and seeking themselves. God knew their end just like He knew their beginning. God knew what they would change and what they would not. We need to learn our ways are different from God's ways. He has the ultimate reason for all things. He holds the plans and the future, but He allows us the choice.

Proverbs 18:21 NIV ^{21} *The tongue has the power of life and death, and those who love it will eat its fruit.*

If you have been speaking bad over your children's behavior or simply claiming what you see them do. Know that it has been faith filled. You say they are selfish, and guess what? They are. Take the challenge with yourself and begin to speak life over them. If you want great respectful children. Do your part and let God do His. Didn't He teach you (His Child) to train your children in the way they should go then when they are old, they will not depart from it. You do not have to believe in them. Stop putting your faith in them. You will be let down each time. Start putting your faith in God. Start applying His word in that belief and watch change happen. Decide to speak life. Use your shield of faith and protect your children. That is your divine power.

James 3:9-12 With the tongue we praise our Lord and Father, and with it we curse human beings, who have been made in God's likeness. 10 Out of the same mouth come praise and cursing. My brothers and sisters, this should not be. 11 Can both fresh water and salt water flow from the same spring? 12 My brothers and sisters, can a fig tree bear olives, or a grapevine bear figs? Neither can a salt spring produce fresh water.

Decide this day who you will serve with your actions and reactions. Pick up your shield of faith and fight the enemy for your children. Ask Jesus for wisdom and understanding. Then begin to fast. Did you know a fast is not just with food? A fast can be pushing aside the plate of aggravation, control, pity, defense. These things we will call vegetables. Don't you want a fast finally from vegetables? We will choose fruits over vegetables any day. Jesus says you cannot plant a grapevine and get figs, right? You cannot plant corn (worry, control, pity, stress, speaking death) and get bananas (hope, joy, peace, love, self-control). Decide from this point on when your child does something that is not of God. That you will speak life into them. It looks like this.

1. Jake: How is Sally? Is she still in jail.
   You: Yes, but God is working on her I been praying for Him to send a servant to reach her.
   Notes: Do not start crying (to show poor me, or poor Sally). Do not say she will never do what is right. Because guess what, you will continue to call this on her. She needs the prayer warrior in you that God just called out to apply

God's word and intercede for her.

2. Mary: How are you feeling?
   You: My back is hurting but I been in prayer, and I am hopeful in God to heal it. I will do what I can do while God does what He does.
   Notes: Do not say, Oh my back is hurting I do not know what to do. I guess I just deserve this.

Decide you want the power from God by using the divine power He has given you. Do not seek pity over power. Pity is a weapon the devil gave to you. He has convinced you it will help you get by. It will help you to get things done by others. This weapon will give you attention because you are in need. God gives us divine weapons to fight these battles. These battles are won when we use His shield of faith. When we decide we are going to be healed because God says so. Then we can do all things through Christ Jesus that strengthens us.

Challenge : Decide to pick up your shield of faith. Decide that you will speak life over your circumstances Decide you know that life will happen because God has promised you this.

Scripture: Learn this scripture. Put it on an index card by your bed, in your vehicle, on your desk and make it a point to say it until you know it. Say it until you believe it. Say it until you show it.

Ephesians 4:29 NIV²⁹ Do not let any unwholesome talk come out of your mouths, but only what is helpful for building others up according to their needs, that it may benefit those who listen.

Application: This is how you activate your shield, verse, and awareness that you need to trust in Jesus first, not yourself and not others. You do this by saying and claiming this verse instead of the complaining, cussing, gossiping, and controlling.

Prayer : Lord let no unwholesome talk come out of my mouth. Help me to only edify you and others in Jesus name amen.

Receive: Say Lord I receive a changed tongue. I receive that I will edify you in my actions and reactions. I receive that I will speak life, not death over others in Jesus name amen.

Write down who or what you speak death into. Then write down how you can speak life into them. Make a goal to speak life every time something goes wrong with this person, place, or thing. This will be your fast. Then watch God manifest abundance in you and around you as your faith increases. You will have this to look back to later when another person, place, or thing comes around that seems to want to defeat you. You will have your own HOPE that God is

ARMOR UP

able. That hope is your divine power too. Use your weapons. Win these battles.

SAY IT: *John 8:36 NIV 36 So if the Son sets you free, you will be free indeed.*

PRAY IT: *Lord the son sets me free so I am free indeed in Jesus name amen.*

CHAPTER 5

Your Helmet of Salvation

Ephesians 2:8-9 NIV 8 For it is by grace you have been saved, through faith—and this is not from yourselves, it is the gift of God—9 not by works, so that no one can boast.

You cannot earn salvation! You simply turn to salvation! There is a huge difference. Earning is to work for it. Earning is to deserve it. You do not deserve salvation. You cannot take the credit for your salvation. Salvation is a gift from God. Jesus Christ died for you to have salvation. Jesus loves you, and His hope is in you. Jesus chose you. Many have rejected you. Now you may be feeling unworthy to be saved. Jesus wants you to know many rejected Him too. Sadly, many still do. Sadly, one of them may have or still is you. Remember we trust in Him with action. You may wonder how an action is different from works. You take the action to turn to salvation. To turn from the old you, to the new you. To turn from the world and to Jesus. You cannot do ABC (A. Change your old habits. B. Stop sinning C. Put on a suit to look the part). You simply decide you need Jesus to help you with everything, because you know you cannot do it alone.

You may have been taught you were born with salvation. You may have been taught all are chosen. You may have been taught once saved always saved. Today you will learn none of that is true. If you think Jesus is going to allow the sweet old lady that gossips on the porch all day long into heaven, you are wrong. To Gossip is a sin and is fueled with hate and evil thoughts. Being cute, funny, or old will not get her the free pass. Jesus seeks the heart. He would have let the devil stay in heaven, think about it. Pride is no different than gossip in the eyes of the Lord. He shares with us in Romans 1 sin is sin. He also does not say in the bible that there are only 7 deadly sins. That is a religious lie too.

Romans 1: 29-32 NIV - They have become filled with every kind of wickedness, evil, greed and depravity. They are full of envy, murder, strife, deceit and malice. They are gossips, 30 slanderers, God-haters, insolent, arrogant and boastful; they invent ways of doing evil; they disobey their parents; 31 they have no understanding, no fidelity, no love, no mercy. 32 Although they know God's righteous decree that those who do such things deserve death, they not only continue to do these very things but also approve of those who practice them.

Notice there is not a 123 order, sin is sin. This may have some feeling defeated. God will show you in John 3:16-17 that this is not what Jesus wants. Jesus died for you because He knew He needed to make that sacrifice because of our temptations of the flesh. However, He does not expect us to use His grace and mercy as some sort of free life pass. We are not in a video game. This is real life. But this is where God's mercy and grace steps in. Jesus teaches us He sees our heart. Which means, He knows our motives. He knows when we sin because we are inexcusable or if we are striving daily to seek Him. Truly only you and God know this about you. You can fake it all you want to others, but God knows.

John 3:16 NIV 16 For God so loved the world that he gave his one and only Son, that whoever believes in him shall not perish but have eternal life. 17 For God did not send his Son into the world to condemn the world, but to save the world through him.

Many like verse 16 because they think, or they are taught' " I am saved WHOO Hoo". This is not true. Again, believe is an action word. If you are not showing you believe in God, then you do not truly believe in God. Jesus gives you verse 17 to ensure you He did not come to send you to hell. He came to save you from it. He came so that His word would bring you wisdom and understanding to set you free. Your ultimate divine weapon is salvation. So, learn to put this covering on. Learn this helmet will protect your mind.

Proverbs 23:7 NKJV ⁷For as he thinks in his heart, so is he. "Eat and drink!" he says to you, But his heart is not with you.

    This means your mind and heart is the operation of your actions and reactions. They are the control center for your soul. The things in your heart process through your mind and come out of your motives. If you put on the helmet of salvation each morning things will change for you. You will bring awareness to your heart and mind that you want to be like Christ. You will remember you have the helmet of salvation on.

    You can begin to pray for repentance and awareness of sin. Lord give me awareness when I am about to sin and give me the courage not to sin in Jesus name amen. The Holy Spirit will then prompt you even more with a sensitive spirit just before you sin. You will go to cuss someone out and you will feel that tug from the Holy Spirit in that split second. Then you will resist the devil, or you will blurt out whatever the devil prompted you to say. You see the devil gives you his weapons. They look like cussing, gossip, slander, defense, offense. Are you picking up his weapons and fighting with the world? Do you want to use the weapons of divine power from God that look like love, joy, peace, faithfulness, gentleness, goodness, kindness, and self-control.

    The devil may have made you believe those weapons are weak.

But God will assure you they are not. Jesus is the way, the truth, and the life. He is the only way to fight the battles of this world because they truly are not battles with flesh. The battles are with spirits, and you have the divine power to demolish strongholds, and the choice to use them.

Ephesians 6:12 NIV [12] *For our struggle is not against flesh and blood, but against the rulers, against the authorities, against the powers of this dark world and against the spiritual forces of evil in the heavenly realms.*

The only way to win is with Jesus. The only way is to fight with the spiritual weapons He gives us. The only way to stay protected is by putting on Jesus. Take the time in the morning to say I am putting on the helmet of salvation. As you are brushing your hair say this. You will be more aware that Jesus is in you, on you, and with you. That is all the protection you will need. You will begin to show in your actions and reactions that you know He is present. You will start to watch what you say as if He were that grandparent or teacher, you would not dare speak bad things in front of. You tend to say and do things you want to do. This is because you have no awareness in your conscious that Jesus is right there. Put Jesus on and speak to Him each morning and throughout the day. You will gain a great awareness then your mind, mouth, and motives will reflect that awareness.

You will notice less things bother you. You will notice you go to God first before yourself, social media, or others. You will begin to notice your way, truth, and life change reflects Jesus. Others will start to notice your transformation. You will begin to hear others say the things about you that you been trying to fake so long. They will become real and true because Jesus will be shining through you.

Acts 2: 36 -39 NIV "Therefore let all Israel be assured of this: God has made this Jesus, whom you crucified, both Lord and Messiah." 37 When the people heard this, they were cut to the heart and said to Peter and the other apostles, "Brothers, what shall we do?" 38 Peter replied, "Repent and be baptized, every one of you, in the name of Jesus Christ for the forgiveness of your sins. And you will receive the gift of the Holy Spirit. 39 The promise is for you and your children and for all who are far off—for all whom the Lord our God will call."

It is important not just to know and hold on to verse 38 like most do. Verses 36-39 pack the whole truth together. Paul is teaching here that we must repent and be baptized in Jesus name. Why? Because no one gets to the Father except through Jesus Christ. Meaning you will not get to Heaven without salvation. Meaning you will not get to Heaven without being baptized in Jesus name. Meaning you will not get to Heaven without applying the word of God in your life. God showed you the way, truth, and life when He walked on this earth in the flesh as Jesus Christ. Jesus is our advocate, our mediator, our savior. So, what if a person just became saved and did not know of baptism, or did not have the chance to be baptized? Just like the thief on the cross next to Jesus at the time of the crucifixion, Jesus knew His heart and took Him too. Why, because He repented. Jesus always makes a way if our heart is sincere. Praying for the person after death will not help. Saying that person is a beautiful angel in heaven will not make them there. Teaching them about Jesus while they are here will allow them to go to Jesus because they will meet Jesus in you. Do your part with your weapon. If you love them, tell them about Jesus. Let them have salvation too and know how to receive it.

Have you ever been in a car accident and just before you hit the object it seemed like things were in slow motion. I believe that is God giving you grace and mercy. That little time slot to call out to Him with your weapon of salvation. Not your weapon from the devil saying O xxxx (cuss words). What is in your heart will come out of your mouth. Make sure you are eating of Jesus. This means make sure you are reading His word. This will allow you to identify Him speaking to you more. This will bring awareness of His presence. This will help you activate salvation by simply going to the helmet and putting it on. Having the helmet in your closet or on your dresser will not help you. You must put it on.

Look at your body like a bucket of water. Picture it filled to the top with water (Jesus). If there is no room to take in anything else because you are filled. Then the dirt and trash that may come around can only fall on the surface of the water. If you are constantly pouring

ARMOR UP

in water (Jesus) , then the trash and dirt will flow right off the top and be washed out. If you let that bucket begin to get low. The first place it will be empty is the top, right? Your top is your head, your mind. The first place the trash and dirt are going to try to land on would be in your mind. If you keep the helmet on of salvation you will not be conformed to the world. You will constantly be transformed by the renewing of the mind. You will hear the temptation (dirt/trash) and you will hear the word of God. Then you will have the choice each time to make up your mind.

Write down the things that seem to be your trash and dirt. What seems to constantly come to your mind. Is it that time someone hurt you. Is it fear of a cheating spouse. Is it your concern to pass a test. Then pick a book in the bible. I will suggest the book of James, but if God shows you another follow His lead, not mine.

Challenge : Decide to put on your helmet of salvation. When you are getting dressed and putting on your hat or brushing your hair. Say forgive me Lord for my sins and give me more awareness of my sins. Give me the courage to not sin. I am putting on my helmet of salvation that you gave to me in Jesus name amen.

Scripture: Learn this scripture. Put it on an index card by your bed, in your vehicle, on your desk and make it a point to say it until you know it. Say it until you believe it. Say it until you show it.

Jill Deville

2 Timothy 1:7 NKJV⁷ For God has not given us a spirit of fear, but of power and of love and of a sound mind.

Application: Put on your helmet each morning while repenting of your sins and ask God to give you wisdom, understanding and courage not to sin.

Prayer : Lord you did not give me a spirit of fear, you gave me a spirit of love, power and sound mind in Jesus name amen.

Receive: Say Lord I receive love, power and a sound mind in Jesus name amen.

When you or others upset you pray this : Lord, you did not give us a spirit of fear, you gave us a spirit of love, power and sound mind in Jesus name amen. Know that the person that done wrong needs the prayer and know that you need the prayer too for the way you feel about it. I call it a invite. It is an invite from Jesus because He trust you to pray for them. Because He knows that you know His word and that you will show it in your actions and reactions. He needs you as His prayer warrior. Trade your fear for faith. Trade your confusion for wisdom. Use your divine weapon from God. Put on this helmet.

ARMOR UP

SAY IT: *Romans 12:2 NKJV² And do not be conformed to this world, but be transformed by the renewing of your mind, that you may prove what is that good and acceptable and perfect will of God.*

PRAY IT: *Lord I will not conform to the world I will be transformed to the renewing of the mind to prove you have power that is good, and acceptable and perfect in Jesus name amen.*

CHAPTER 6

Use Your Sword

Hebrews 4:12 NKJV ¹² For the word of God is living and powerful, and sharper than any two-edged sword, piercing even to the division of soul and spirit, and of joints and marrow, and is a discerner of the thoughts and intents of the heart.

Your sword, the word of God should be the weapon of choice in all circumstances. The word of God is your weapon, your instructions, your road map to Heaven. The word of God is living and active. The word of God speaks to you when you are in need. When you read the word of God daily you will hear God loudly in everything. You will be watching a movie and see it as a parable. You will be speaking to someone and hear exactly what to say or how to help them. The living word becomes living inside of you and active. The word of God reaches and teaches to the depths of your bones.

ARMOR UP

The word of God helps you to discern all people, places, and things. The word of God also discerns you. It is a sharp sword that can kill and destroy anything that comes near you that is not of God. It will cut away sin. It will cut away friends and family. It will cut away anything that God knows will hinder your growth with Him.

God will give us the warnings to allow us to choose to walk away, get away, or make a change. He will do this with jobs, relationships, health, wealth or the lack there of. The warnings look like strife. They feel like that gut wrenching feeling like you do not belong at this party, at this job, with this person. You will see it in your relationships with control, worry, stress, cheating, beatings and more. You will see the warning with health issues when you not taking care of yourself properly. God wants us to get enough of something and make a choice with our own free will.

Also, as the loving parent Jesus is. He will also step in and say enough. If you will not cut them away with your divine weapon (choice) from me. Then I will work on them, or it to be removed from you. Yes, it hurts, but it saves your life eternally. It moves the person, place, or thing out of your way. Jesus does this so that you can have the plans He chose for you.

Many have been convinced or even taught that they can not understand the bible. That is a lie from the devil. You can understand it. There are even versions that help break it down more for you. You just need to know from someone that has been studying which version is the best read. I personally would suggest NKJV first. If you see it is hard, compare it with a NIV or NLT version in hand or online to help break down some of the larger words.

When my daughter was learning she had the NKJV in hand and her children's bible (also NKJV) in hand. It helped her to use as a cross reference. Do not feel stupid purchasing or using a children's bible. Let me tell you why. Let's say you been a Christian for 6 months, or even 3 years. Why would someone hand a baby a NKJV bible that has not learned how to read yet. The pictures and the simplicity in the children's bible will stimulate your mind. It will help you to comprehend more. Jesus also teaches us in Matthew 18 to come to Him like a child.

God's word will teach you the most. However how will you understand without a teacher. That is why it is important to go to God's house to learn more about the word of God. That is a great place to go get your sword. Especially if you were not given that sword when you were born naturally or spiritually.

We did come with an instruction manual. It has all the directions on how to put us together. It has a treasure map to get to our inheritance. It has a road map to get to Heaven. It is packed with examples to get the full picture for the finished product. However, some are not handed that instruction manual at our natural or spiritual birth. For some we store it on the table, or in a drawer. We prefer to just look at the big picture to put things together. Much like when you get that great big playhouse or bike, then you just toss the instructions and look at the pictures. You end up with so many pieces missing.

ARMOR UP

You think you do not need them. Until later you find out you really did. The picture of other Christians does not look like you. We all have our own design.

Jesus assigns people He ordains, orders, and trusts to teach us. If you refuse those teachings, then you are saying He did not pick the right person for you. Think on that a moment. Also consider you walked in or followed someone in haste to a church due to your people pleasing skills. Now you are not in the place God instructed you to be. So, you feel out of place and want to blame others for it. You have a choice. You also need to know what God joins together no man (not even you) can separate. Therefore, if you are feeling some sort of way then ask the following: 1. Am I here to be the light in the darkness. 2. Am I hear to show the word of God in my actions and reactions to be the billboard for Jesus. 3. Did I come here in haste or in people pleasing. Do I need to excuse myself and pray to see where God wants me.

Many go to a certain church because their family, friends, and traditions say that is where you need to be. They stay so uncomfortable that they feel something is wrong with them. No one else seems to be uncomfortable, why am I? God wants you to ask Him where you should go. Maybe you do not want to ask because you do not want to upset your friends, family or look odd to your town? You rather go to hell, upset or reject God than look bad to others. Understand you are where you want to be, you have a choice. Maybe it was because they have a religion, and you feel if you do 123 then

ABC will happen. Maybe it is because you want to be lost and not accountable. Maybe it is because you like to follow people and not God. Examine your why and ask God how to address that why.

Others choose not to go to church because they were judged, rejected, cast out, ridiculed, controlled, manipulated. I would say this is all good reasons. That excuse is so lame. First, Jesus dealt with all this too. See the book of Matthew. He showed you what to do when this happens. Rejecting Him and all churches was not it. He did not hurt you. All churches did not do this to you. You seem to use this excuse for God and church only. Let me show you the truth so that the truth can set you free.

You cannot say you had a pleasant experience at a store, restaurant, with a utility company, or even a person all your life. You tend to still use that service, store, restaurant or engage with that person, right? Why? Because they have things you need. You give them mercy and grace. You even give them all your money, and time. Feeling convicted yet? Good! We need to feel convicted. This is your weapon from God. This is how God broke me. I pray this is how you gain wisdom and understanding too. It saved my life from ignorance and hell. It changed my way of making excuses and looking like a fool. It changed my way of thinking.

When I decided to use my weapon from God (the sword) and cut the mess out of my mouth, motives, and mind. My life began to change. I had finally figured out how to use my sword. This weapon allows you to cut to the truth like Jesus. You will begin to see and discern things differently.

A stall on the highway will now look like protection. A call when you busy will not look like an invite. A loss of work will now look like an opportunity. A health scare will now look like healing. Your mind begins to shift because you decided to use your sword to cut out the enemies' schemes. You also used this sword to cut out the excuses, the lies, the deceit. Finally, you decided to use the sword to cut out the old ways. You decided to demolish strongholds not only for you, but for the good of many in your path and in your generations to come.

Romans 10:14-15 NIV [14] How, then, can they call on the one they have not believed in? And how can they believe in the one of whom they have not heard? And how can they hear without someone preaching to them? [15] And how can anyone preach unless they are sent? As it is written: "How beautiful are the feet of those who bring good news!"[a]

God is teaching you hear to go to the teachers, preachers, pastors He trust to teach you. If you do not feel like you are receiving and growing, then pray for God to lead you where He wants you to be. You do not have to insult anyone. You do not have to make a scene. God does not need you to protect or defend Him. He is looking to see if you will do what His word says. Will you use His sword and rightly divide what to do. God is teaching you in this scripture. If the teacher appointed to teach you is in right standing with Him. You will see it in their walk. No, they will not be perfect, ever. They are human flesh too. They will constantly seek perfection, which is Jesus. They will constantly direct you to Jesus and not themselves. You will feel Jesus from them. You will never feel hell or the devil from them if they are from God.

No matter what. Read in 1 and 2 Samuel about King Saul and David. David will teach you to never go against someone God ordained even when they have lost their anointing because of their disobedience to God. You will see this with King Saul. No matter what he did David, David done what was right. He knew He was not accountable to King Saul. He knew he was accountable to God. Trust me in the natural King Saul would look like he deserved death. He did horrible things, especially to David. That was God's decision to make, not David's. God showed us in this message to not go against His chosen. Otherwise, God will come after you. Let me encourage you to read 1 and 2 Samuel.

It is so important to read the word of God. You will learn that everything you go through is written in there. With a solution, example and so much more help you be a Christian. To stop making excuses and stop being lost. Jesus wants you to have freedom on earth. Jesus wants you to have peace and joy. Jesus wants you to enjoy all the great things that is available to you in this world. He just does not want you to become of the world.

ARMOR UP

Jesus does not want you on this strict religious schedule with no joy, hope, or money. He wants and has abundance for you. He is just waiting for you to get out your sword and cut Him in to the front of your line. There is no way to learn the word of God without reading it. There is no way to hear God and know it is Him without knowing the word of God. God even says how will they know the word of God without a teacher. Jesus wants you to be in unity with others. Do you know why?

You can feel Jesus through true Christians when they hug you, shake your hand and pat you on the back. You can see Jesus in true Christians when they speak to you with love, and God's word. You will witness Jesus is there for you when other Christians show up. You may have just begged your family, friends or that person you are always there for to attend something that means allot to you. Then you look in the crowd and they are not there. But that Christian is, or that person you least expected is there. Why is that?

It is because you will know it is Jesus if it is unexpected. If it is a person, you did not beg, control, manipulate or even sow into with a good heart. You are expecting them. So, you will not see Jesus. You will see them. Jesus uses the sword to cut through the chaos of our mind. He wants you to know He is there. He wants you to know He cares. When you begin to trust in Him with those people you try to pressure or expect things from; then He will begin to work on them to show up. That way when they finally do. You will see Him in them too. That is divine power. That is how you use your weapons to see ahead and fight with God's power and authority.

You will hear Jesus through fellow Christians. You will feel and witness His power in worship with unity of others. Now this part, you may not like so much. You need to be in unity with other Christians to show what you know. Especially when others do not show what they know. That is how you will know that you truly know God's word and believe it. You will do it. Your weapon, that sword is powerful. Doing God's word is powerful. It is one thing to know it, it is another to show it. Knowing who someone is, is not the same as knowing them, right? God knows you can be the best Christian all by yourself. God knows you can be the best Christian to your friends and people that do for you. God wants to see what you going to do with your enemies. God speaks allot of this in His word.

Luke 6:32-36 NKJV *[32] "But if you love those who love you, what credit is that to you? For even sinners love those who love them. [33] And if you do good to those who do good to you, what credit is that to you? For even sinners do the same. [34] And if you lend to those from whom you hope to receive back, what credit is that to you? For even sinners lend to sinners to receive as much back. [35] But love your enemies, do good, and lend, [a] hoping for nothing in return; and your reward will be great, and you will be sons of the Most High. For He is kind to the unthankful and evil. [36] Therefore be merciful, just as your Father also is merciful.*

ARMOR UP

Most do not want to read the word of God because they know and have heard, if you know it you must show it. God knows that you have common sense. You know right from wrong. If not from the commandments, you hear it in the laws. No matter what you must choose a side. The devil has convinced you that you do not like to read. Well even the world has come up with an audible bible. Listen to it. Start somewhere. The devil has made you believe you do not have time to read the bible. But somehow you have time to binge tv, games and socials. Let's not forget all the time you spend complaining when you could be reading to hear how to fix whatever you been complaining about. God's word is active. When you are dealing with something. No matter where you go in the bible to read. God will answer you through that reading. It is a huge weapon. The sword gives you so much divine power.

The sword is the way you know that you hear God. It gives you the wisdom and understanding you need when you need it. The sword should always stay with you. If not physically in your hand, then hold it in your heart from what you have read. The devil may have convinced you that you can not remember anything so why read it. This verse is for you.

John 14:26 NIV But the Advocate, the Holy Spirit, whom the Father will send in my name, will teach you all things and will remind you of everything I have said to you.

Ask the Holy Spirit to remind you and He will. It is that simple. It is that faith we were speaking of with the shield of faith. You should already have that shield in hand. Therefore, you know to activate your faith and how. If saying, " I can not read, I can not comprehend, I am confused, I do not have time" worked in that faith. Because you chose to use the devil's weapons to say those things. Now those things have manifested that truth. Then why would God's weapons and truth not manifest all the same if you put your faith in Him. Use His weapons by speaking life. Pick up your shield of faith and your sword (the word of God) and use your divine weapons.

You have the armor, and you have the weapons. This book is giving you the wisdom and understanding only because it is prayed over and powered up by God's anointing to help you. These are things God has shown me in my time with Him. This is the armor and weapons God gave me to fight whatever came my way. God is the only one that can and will protect, provide, heal, defend, correct, love, and save us. Sometimes He does it directly and sometimes He does it indirectly through an obedient child of God. He even showed us that He can and will work through an enemy like Pilot, the king of Daniel, and others. When Daniel decided He was armored and protected by God, the enemy believed because of His faith. The enemy even prayed and fasted for Daniel. When Christ stood firm with Pilot, knowing God had the plan and the outcome. Pilot done as God instructed even though it appeared evil to us all. It was God's plan not Pilot's.

Reading the word of God and knowing the circumstances and

outcome through the stories gives us hope. Hope is a divine power. Hope is a great weapon. It allows you to fight stress, worry and fear. Decide to use your weapons from God and pick up your sword and use it.

Challenge : This week before you pick up your phone, pick up your sword (bible). When you open your eyes in the morning say Hello Lord, hand me my sword. Before you go to bed at night say Goodnight Lord and clean your sword (read the word). Thank God for that sword and all that it killed and destroyed for you that day.

Scripture: Learn this scripture. Put it on an index card by your bed, in your vehicle, on your desk and make it a point to say it until you know it. Say it until you believe it. Say it until you show it.

John 10:10 NIV The thief comes only to steal and kill and destroy; I have come that they may have life, and have it to the full.

Application: Make time to pick up your sword and read it. Then take the time to do it. (Show What You Know)

Prayer : Lord I choose to no longer allow the devil to kill, steal and destroy me, I want the life in abundance you have for me to the full in Jesus name amen.

Receive: Say Lord I receive your abundance to the full for me and all that I know and come in contact with in Jesus name amen.

This week decide to pick a book of the bible and read it. God is looking for quality time with you. Not quantity. He does not want this experience to be a check list. He wants you to read, ask Him questions and speak to Him about the word you are reading.

Take a scripture, read it. Then write down what you received from it. Write down your questions you have about it. Ask God how it can apply to you. Ask God to give you wisdom on how to apply it to your life. Ask the Holy Spirit to remind you of the scripture when you need it for your circumstance or for others. Writing helps the mind comprehend and receive. It also helps you remember.

ARMOR UP

SAY IT: John 14:26 NIV But the Advocate, the Holy Spirit, whom the Father will send in my name, will teach you all things and will remind you of everything I have said to you.

PRAY IT: Lord I know you sent the Holy Spirit as my advocate to teach me and remind me, Thank you Lord in Jesus name amen.

CHAPTER 7

ARMOR UP

2 Corinthians 10:4-6 Amplified Bible **⁴** *The weapons of our warfare are not physical [weapons of flesh and blood]. Our weapons are divinely powerful for the destruction of fortresses.* **⁵** *We are destroying sophisticated arguments and every exalted and proud thing that sets itself up against the [true] knowledge of God, and we are taking every thought and purpose captive to the obedience of Christ,* **⁶** *being ready to punish every act of disobedience, when your own obedience [as a church] is complete.*

This scripture could be the entire chapter, the very ending of this book. It sums up the entire book. God's ways are not like our ways. We have learned traditions. Like the way we take out the trash, clean our house, speak to others, follow certain sports. We have learned in religion if you do this, this will happen. Whether that "this" was a good or bad thing. We think if we say ten "our Fathers" then our sins will be forgiven. We think if we show up to church that will make God happy. We think if we ask for forgiveness one time then you can do whatever you want because of God's mercy and grace you will go to heaven no matter what. I pray this book helps you to know that is truly not God's ways. That is all man-made ways.

Mark 7 5- 13 NIV 5 So the Pharisees and teachers of the law asked Jesus, "Why don't your disciples live according to the tradition of the elders instead of eating their food with defiled hands?" [6] He replied, "Isaiah was right when he prophesied about you hypocrites; as it is written: "'These people honor me with their lips, but their hearts are far from me. [7] They worship me in vain; their teachings are merely human rules.'[b] [8] You have let go of the commands of God and are holding on to human traditions." [9] And he continued, "You have a fine way of setting aside the commands of God in order to observe[c] your own traditions! [10] For Moses said, 'Honor your father and mother,'[d] and, 'Anyone who curses their father or mother is to be put to death.'[e] [11] But you say that if anyone declares that what might have been used to help their father or mother is Corban (that is, devoted to God)— [12] then you no longer let them do anything for their father or mother. [13] Thus you nullify the word of God by your tradition that you have handed down. And you do many things like that."

Jesus is not looking for traditions, or religion. Jesus is wanting a relationship with you. Jesus gives us a field. That field is not a battlefield. That field is meant to plant crops in. Those crops should look like the fruit of the spirit. Those crops are your weapons of divine power. Those crops will attract others to come to Jesus when they are hungry. Because they will know they will be filled.

Galatians 5:22-23 NKJV *²² But the fruit of the Spirit is love, joy, peace, longsuffering, kindness, goodness, faithfulness, ²³ [a]gentleness, self-control. Against such there is no law.*

Decide to use your field as the harvest. Decide when you are in that field to put on the full armor of God.

Ephesians 6:10-18 NIV The Armor of God ¹⁰ Finally, be strong in the Lord and in his mighty power. ¹¹ Put on the full armor of God, so that you can take your stand against the devil's schemes. ¹² For our struggle is not against flesh and blood, but against the rulers, against the authorities, against the powers of this dark world and against the spiritual forces of evil in the heavenly realms. ¹³ Therefore put on the full armor of God, so that when the day of evil comes, you may be able to stand your ground, and after you have done everything,

ARMOR UP

to stand. <u>*¹⁴ Stand firm then, with the belt of truth buckled around your waist, with the breastplate of righteousness in place,*</u> *¹⁵ and* <u>*with your feet fitted with the readiness that comes from the gospel of peace.*</u> *¹⁶ In addition to all this,* <u>*take up the shield of faith,*</u> *with which you can extinguish all the flaming arrows of the evil one. ¹⁷* <u>*Take the helmet of salvation*</u> *and* <u>*the sword of the Spirit,*</u> *which is the word of God.*
<u>*¹⁸ And pray in the Spirit on all occasions*</u> *with all kinds of prayers and requests. With this in mind, be alert and always keep on praying for all the Lord's people.*

Stand firm with child-like faith and put on your armor of God. This will allow you to have awareness that God is all over you, and in you. You will begin to walk with courage. You will begin to act with confidence. You will begin to activate the fruits of the spirit within you that God has already given you.

How do you feel putting on the armor of God will assist you?

Jill Deville

PUT ON JESUS EVERYDAY
Here is how you put on the armor of God.

1. Undergarments: I am putting on your belt of truth. I want to speak of your word today and resist the lies of the devil.

2. Shirt : Lord I am putting on your breastplate, I know I will be fully protected all day with this on.

3. Pants: I am putting on your shield of faith. I know, I expect, and I hope in your provision in my life.

4. Socks: I am putting on your armored boots. I know they will help me to walk in your way, your truth, and your life.

5. Shoes: I am taking my shield of faith. I am choosing to walk by faith and not by sight.

6. Brush Hair / put on Hat : I am putting on the helmet of salvation. Lord, please forgive me for my sins and give me wisdom and courage not to sin in Jesus name amen.

7. Brushing teeth: Lord clean my mouth, motives, and mind. (pick a set of scriptures) Memorize them and say them while brushing your teeth. Until you can memorize them, put them by the sink. This will not only clean your teeth it will clean your mind, mouth, and motives. This is one way you can pray in the spirit with all kinds of prayers.

CHAPTER 8

Activate Your Weapons

These next set of scriptures are showing how God's faithful warriors were faced with a huge battle. A battle they knew they could not win with their weapons of the world. The battle was too huge. The warriors were too strong. The number of warriors were more than they had. By facts, it looked like they were defeated. It looked like they should surrender. Do you feel like that today with a bill, child, spouse, teacher, pastor, or job? These faith-filled men had weapons of divine power too. These faithful warriors of God chose to use the divine weapons; let's see if they won the battle.

{Do not get caught up on how to pronounce the names in theses verses. Just say a name that starts with that first letter. Especially if you a beginner in reading the word. Yes, the names are important. You will have time to circle back and address that later. Say a name like Keith instead of *Kohathites* that way your focus does not get off the point.}

Jill Deville

2 Chronicles 20:10 NIV "But now here are men from Ammon, Moab and Mount Seir, whose territory you would not allow Israel to invade when they came from Egypt; so they turned away from them and did not destroy them. 11 See how they are repaying us by coming to drive us out of the possession you gave us as an inheritance. 12 Our God, will you not judge them? For we have no power to face this vast army that is attacking us. We do not know what to do, but our eyes are on you." 13 All the men of Judah, with their wives and children and little ones, stood there before the Lord. 14 Then the Spirit of the Lord came on Jahaziel son of Zechariah, the son of Benaiah, the son of Jeiel, the son of Mattaniah, a Levite and descendant of Asaph, as he stood in the assembly. 15 He said: "Listen, King Jehoshaphat and all who live in Judah and Jerusalem!
This is what the Lord says to you: 'Do not be afraid or discouraged because of this vast army. For the battle is not yours, but God's. 16 Tomorrow march down against them. They will be climbing up by the Pass of Ziz, and you will find them at the end of the gorge in the Desert of Jeruel. 17 You will not have to fight this battle. Take up your positions; stand firm and see the deliverance the Lord will give you, Judah and Jerusalem. Do not be afraid; do not be discouraged. Go out to face them tomorrow, and the Lord will be with you.'" 18 Jehoshaphat bowed down with his face to the ground, and all the people of Judah and Jerusalem fell down in worship before
the Lord. 19 Then some Levites from the Kohathites and Korahites stood up and praised the Lord, the God of Israel, with a very loud voice. 20 Early in

the morning they left for the Desert of Tekoa. As they set out, Jehoshaphat stood and said, "Listen to me, Judah and people of Jerusalem! Have faith in the Lord your God and you will be upheld; have faith in his prophets and you will be successful." 21 After consulting the people, Jehoshaphat appointed men to sing to the Lord and to praise him for the splendor of his[c] holiness as they went out at the head of the army, saying: "Give thanks to the Lord, for his love endures forever." 22 As they began to sing and praise, the Lord set ambushes against the men of Ammon and Moab and Mount Seir who were invading Judah, and they were defeated. 23 The Ammonites and Moabites rose up against the men from Mount Seir to destroy and annihilate them. After they finished slaughtering the men from Seir, they helped to destroy one another. 24 When the men of Judah came to the place that overlooks the desert and looked toward the vast army, they saw only dead bodies lying on the ground; no one had escaped. 25 So Jehoshaphat and his men went to carry off their plunder, and they found among them a great amount of equipment and clothing[d] and also articles of value—more than they could take away. There was so much plunder that it took three days to collect it. 26 On the fourth day they assembled in the Valley of Berakah, where they praised the Lord. This is why it is called the Valley of Berakah[e] to this day.

These warriors decided to use prayer, worship, and faith. Can you do that today? Reflect on this battle and know that it is not impossible to win. Take the time to write down a battle you facing that seems impossible to address or fight on your own. Then decide while writing you will pray, worship, and thank God that this battle is His not yours.

ARMOR UP

ACTIVATE YOUR DIVINE WEAPONS

Take a verse a day, week, month, or year. Write it down on index cards, or sticky notes and place it where you will see them. Such as where you are brush your teeth, by your bed, where you watch T.V., or when you get in your vehicle. This is how I learned them. I took one a month. I learned it, I studied it, I learned how to receive it, then I learned how to apply it in my life. Then I fought my battles with it.

In this chapter you will learn how to do the following:

1. How to memorize the verses.
2. What the verse means.
3. The importance of the memorizing the verse.
4. How to recognize when to use the verse.
5. How to access the verse.
6. How to pray the verse.

Treat this next section like a devotional. Work on it at your own pace. You will find knowing, and praying these verses is the best way to pray. Saying and praying your promises from God calls those promises into existence. Sometimes we pray for things selfishly. Sometimes we pray against people thinking we have no part in it, or that only they could be wrong. Pray scriptures (your promises / weapons /armor) instead of your wants and needs in the heat of the moment. That shows your faith in Jesus. It also gives you way more abundance in your answers and faster results.

Jill Deville

Corinthians 5:7 NKJV 7 For we walk by faith, not by sight.

No matter what the facts say in your marriage, children, test, jobs, friendships, circumstances, health, wealth, or the lack thereof – you will walk by the facts God has given you. You will walk in faith. You will know and receive that God will fight for you, that you only need to be still. You will know God will provide for you, because He is your Shepard you shall not want. You will know God is your healer, redeemer, savior, protector, defender because His word says so. As you eat (read/receive) God's word. You will begin to believe it in an action and reaction to any battles that comes your way.

What facts of the world are you dealing with? Do your facts say you marriage is in trouble, you are ill, you need more money, you have a horrible job? What is it for you? Decide today that you trust in the Lord. Each time this stress, worry, bad words, or thoughts approach you; say this. I will walk by faith and not by sight in Jesus name amen.

At first you will mess up. Then eventually. you will catch yourself saying or thinking negative things. You will then start to rebuke them and speak by faith. It takes time, but as you put on the armor and use your weapons you will see battles won.

Prayer: Lord I choose to walk by faith and not by sight in Jesus name amen.

ARMOR UP

How did this verse help you?

Jill Deville

Matthew 6:33 NKJV ³³ But seek first the kingdom of God and His righteousness, and all these things shall be added to you.

This verse teaches you to put God first. By now maybe you have put you or others first. You may not know where to begin with this transformation. This section will help you. How do you begin to seek God first and His right standing? When you wake up in the morning, say Good Morning Lord! This allows you to acknowledge Jesus is with you right when you wake up. When you are looking for your clothes, ask Jesus what He thinks you should wear. Ask Him where is that shirt you love that is so cozy. Do this instead of ranting about not knowing what to wear. Do this instead of complaining that you cannot find your shirt. It works much better. When you do not get a text back or an answer on the phone decide that the person is driving, on another call, or busy. Decide this is not a negative thing. Decide to seek God first by reacting in a positive way. When something unexpected happens, or someone tells you off. Decide to seek God first by utilizing your weapons of divine power and be still. This will show God you trust in Him first, and you know He will handle it. This also shows you that you understand He is your protector and defender. He will then prompt you to get the sling shot, or He will handle it for you. Remember He is God. He got this.

Prayer: I will seek you first Lord and your right standing so that all will be added to me in Jesus name amen.

ARMOR UP

How did this verse help you?

Jill Deville

Psalm 23:1 NKJV 23 The Lord is my shepherd; I shall not [a]want.

This verse teaches you that the Lord is your provider. He will provide what you need and want. This one was hard for me to learn until one day it was not. I would like to say it was easy, but it was not at all. I kept trying to reason when something did not go right, or someone did not like me. I would try to work long hours instead of having any time for myself. I did not even want to stop to go to the restroom or eat. When I wanted something nice or to go eat out. I would just use the money I had. Then I would have to work even harder to make that bill money back. I had trouble with tithing and offering. I wondered how I could pay that if I did not even have enough for food or bills. I was showing I was the shepherd, and I definitely was not. Once I learned the Lord is my Shepard I shall not want. I began to go to Him for everything. From needing help with a bill to needing help with a bad hair day. No matter what the want was, I asked Him. I learned the reason I was in want and need was because I was not tithing and offering. His word says once you tithe and offer then He will throw open the floor gates for you. We restrict ourself with our lack of faith. Recently when I went to the zoo with my grandchild I did not want to put on the sunscreen. I hated how it felt. It was so hot. I asked God if he would keep me covered not to burn. It was near 100 degrees, I left there with no sunburn. It does not matter what your want is as long as your intentions are pure. God is

ARMOR UP

always able.

Prayer: Lord you are my Shepherd I shall not want in Jesus name amen.

How did this verse help you?

CHAPTER 9

Holy Spirit Activate

John 14:26 NIV But the Advocate, the Holy Spirit, whom the Father will send in my name, will teach you all things and will remind you of everything I have said to you.

Now it is time to activate the Holy Spirit in you. Take these verses and ask the Holy Spirit to speak, teach, remind, and guide you in them. This chapter will help you to activate discernment, wisdom, courage, understanding, and a will to serve God first. These are very powerful weapons from God. If you take the time to memorize, understand, pray, and activate them in your life you will see a transformation. You will see many spiritual battles won.

In all things, and in all situations, you will begin to hear these verses and you will know that God just handed you the weapon. You will stop taking the weapons the devil tries to give you. You know the ones. They look like defense, anger, aggravation, control, pity, pride. You will now begin to see those are the weak weapons.

ARMOR UP

Exodus 14:14 NIV *¹⁴ The* L*ORD* *will fight for you; you need only to be still."*

What are you receiving from this verse? What does it mean to you?

_____
_____
_____
_____
_____
_____
_____

How can you use this verse (armor / weapon)?

_____
_____
_____
_____
_____
_____
_____
_____
_____

Share how this verse helped you win the battle ?

___

Write In Your Prayer:

___

When you do not know what to say. Say the Lord will first for me I need only to be still. This will help you plant and grow the fruit of **Patience**. Remember your field was meant for crops. The battle is already won.

ARMOR UP

Psalm 91:2 NIV ² I will say of the LORD, "He is my refuge and my fortress, my God, in whom I trust."

What are you receiving from this verse? What does it mean to you?

Go read Psalms 91 the entire chapter. It will show you in depth of what this verse is so important to you to use as your armor and weapon. Then write down the importance of praying and claiming this verse Psalms 91:2

Jill Deville

Share how this verse helped you win the battle?

_____
_____
_____
_____
_____
_____
_____

Write In Your Prayer:

_____
_____
_____
_____
_____

When you get up in the morning and as you go about your day remember to take refuge and why it is so important that you do. This will help you plant and grow the fruit of **Faithfulness**. Remember your field was meant for crops. The battle is already won.

ARMOR UP

Philippians 4:13 NIV **¹³** *I can do all this through him who gives me strength.*

What are you receiving from this verse? What does it mean to you?

_____
_____
_____
_____
_____
_____

How can you use this verse (armor / weapon)?

Example: When I am studying for a test, I can claim this promise. In trying to win a race or reach a goal, I can claim this promise. When climbing a flight of stairs and my knees hurt, I can claim this promise.

_____
_____
_____
_____
_____
_____

Share how this verse helped you win the battle?

Write In Your Prayer:

If you ever feel you cannot do all things through Christ Jesus pull out your bible. Read around this verse. Start with verse ten and then read it through to thirteen. You will notice that you need to be content in the good and the bad, in the want and the abundance. This will help you plant and grow the fruit of **Peace.** Remember your field was meant for crops. The battle is already won.

ARMOR UP

2 Timothy 1:7 NIV ⁷For God has not given us a spirit of fear, but of power and of love and of a sound mind.

What are you receiving from this verse? What does it mean to you ? We covered this verse in this book, reflect to what we spoke on.

_____
_____
_____
_____
_____
_____
_____

How can you use this verse (armor / weapon)?

_____
_____
_____
_____
_____
_____
_____
_____
_____
_____

Jill Deville

Share how this verse helped you win the battle?

_____
_____
_____
_____
_____
_____
_____

Write In Your Prayer:

_____
_____
_____
_____

Remember if you see something that do not like it. If you are going through something and you are uncomfortable. This verse will bring you freedom. Pray this verse and claim this verse over you and the person you are bothered by. It will free both of you from the spiritual attack from the devil. This will help you plant and grow the fruit of **Goodness.** Remember your field was meant for crops. The battle is already won.

ARMOR UP

Luke 10:19 NKJV *[19] Behold, I give you the authority to trample on serpents and scorpions, and over all the power of the enemy, and nothing shall by any means hurt you.*

What are you receiving from this verse? What does it mean to you? Ask what yourself, what does the *serpents and scorpions* represent.

_____
_____
_____
_____
_____
_____
_____
_____

How can you use this verse (armor / weapon)?

_____
_____
_____
_____
_____
_____
_____

Share how this verse helped you win the battle?

Write In Your Prayer:

Know that the enemy only has power over you if you give it to him. He cannot defeat you. Use these weapons of warfare (these scriptures) When you begin to feel the stress, anxiety, anger, pride, control slip in, say no devil. Claim, I have the authority to trample on you with God's promises. This will help you plant and grow the fruit of ***Self-Control.*** Remember your field was meant for crops. The battle is already won.

ARMOR UP

2 Corinthians 5:17 NKJV ¹⁷ *Therefore, if anyone is in Christ, he is a new creation; old things have passed away; behold, all things have become new.*

What are you receiving from this verse? What does it mean to you?

How can you use this verse (armor / weapon)?

Jill Deville

Share how this verse helped you win the battle?

_____
_____
_____
_____
_____
_____

Write In Your Prayer:

_____
_____
_____
_____

When you first begin to turn your life to Christ, you want so badly for others to see the new you. You cannot wait to truly see the new you. In this transition when the devil tries to remind you of the old you directly or indirectly through others. Stand firm and say I do not live there anymore. Why do you keep going to that vacated house. This will help you plant and grow the fruit of *Joy*. Remember your field was meant for crops. The battle is already won.

ARMOR UP

John 8:36 NKJV *³⁶ Therefore if the Son makes you free, you shall be free indeed.*

What are you receiving from this verse? What does it mean to you? How did the son set you free?

_____
_____
_____
_____
_____
_____
_____

How can you use this verse (armor / weapon)?

_____
_____
_____
_____
_____
_____
_____
_____

Jill Deville

Share how this verse helped you win the battle?

_____
_____
_____
_____
_____

Write In Your Prayer:

_____
_____
_____

    Know that Jesus done the hard part already. Know that Jesus was beaten to death, hung on a cross, and died for you. Know that Jesus resurrected for you and now is reconciled in you. You have a piece of Him with you all day, every day. When it feels like you on that cross being beaten with life, know that Jesus is there with you. Jesus gives us freedom in His way, truth, and life. We must remind ourselves; He chose us because He loves us. This will help you plant and grow the fruit of **Love.** Remember your field was meant for crops. The battle is already won.

ARMOR UP

John 3:16 NKJV ¹⁶ *For God so loved the world that He gave His only begotten Son, that whoever believes in Him should not perish but have everlasting life.*

What are you receiving from this verse? What does it mean to you? We covered this verse in this book, reflect to what we spoke on.

How can you use this verse (armor / weapon)?

Jill Deville

Share how this verse helped you win the battle?

_____
_____
_____
_____
_____
_____

Write In Your Prayer:

_____
_____
_____

Jesus died, rose, and lives again with you. Know that He did not do this so you could remain in bondage and in sin. Jesus has endured allot for you. He wanted you to have salvation. Therefore, when you are waiting on someone to turn to Christ, remember the wait Jesus had with you. When you are waiting for a healing or a circumstance to change; remember Jesus waited on you. You were worth His wait. Let Him be worth yours. This will help you plant and grow the fruit of **Longsuffering.** Remember your field was meant for crops. The battle is already won.

ARMOR UP

2 Corinthians 9:6 NKJV *⁶ But this I say: He who sows sparingly will also reap sparingly, and he who sows [a] bountifully will also reap [b] bountifully.*

What are you receiving from this verse? What does it mean to you? Is God just speaking of money? Are could this be time, listening, working, being present, and so much more?

_____
_____
_____
_____
_____
_____
_____
_____

How can you use this verse (armor / weapon)?

_____
_____
_____
_____
_____
_____
_____

Jill Deville

Share how this verse helped you win the battle?

_____

_____

_____

_____

_____

Write In Your Prayer:

_____

_____

_____

Jesus teaches us that whatever we do we should do it for Him. If you truly do everything for Him, you will not grow weary or feel used. If you help someone you will not do it for something in return. You will learn to do, give, serve, listen, answer, work, and more with a cheerful heart. Then God will see you and God will bless you. See Matthew 25:31-46. It will change your life. This will help you plant and grow the fruit of **Kindness.** Remember your field was meant for crops. The battle is already won.

ARMOR UP

Jeremiah 17:14 NKJV ¹⁴ *Heal me, O LORD, and I shall be healed; Save me, and I shall be saved, For You are my praise.*

What are you receiving from this verse? What does it mean to you? Throughout the bible you will see many needs healing, but Jesus prays be saved. Why do you think He said this instead of be healed?

_____
_____
_____
_____
_____
_____
_____
_____

How can you use this verse (armor / weapon)?

_____
_____
_____
_____
_____
_____
_____
_____

Jill Deville

Share how this verse helped you win the battle?

_____
_____
_____
_____
_____

Write In Your Prayer:

_____
_____
_____

Jesus is our healer. Once we realize anything that is not of Him is from the devil, including sickness. When you learn to claim this verse over yourself you will be healed from all that is not of God. When others ask for healing, pray this verse. Why? There may be a deeper sickness behind the flu, soar throat, or cough. Know that God uses signs to get to the root of other things. Most will not ask for prayers until they are sick. When they ask, go all out and ask for them to be saved and healed in Jesus name. This will help you plant and grow in **Healing.** Remember your field was meant for crops. The battle is already won.

ARMOR UP

James 1:22 NKJV ²² *But be doers of the word, and not hearers only, deceiving yourselves.*

What are you receiving from this verse? What does it mean to you?

How can you use this verse (armor / weapon)?

Share how this verse helped you win the battle?

Jill Deville

Write In Your Prayer:

Jesus does not just want us to know of Him. He wants us to know Him and build a relationship with Him. Jesus does not want you to know the word and not do the word. Jesus does not care if you sit in church every Sunday and read 20 chapters a night. Jesus is interested if you are going for Him, and if you going to learn how to do it. This will help you plant and grow in ***Integrity.*** Remember your field was meant for crops. The battle is already won.

CHAPTER 10

Show What You Know

Deuteronomy 5:27 You go near and hear all that the LORD our God may say, and tell us all that the LORD our God says to you, and we will hear and do it.'

The things I share in this book is things that carried me through so many transformations, healings, dark times, and breakthroughs. Without the Word of God, (my sword) I would not have won any of the wars. When I began to read the word of God I read in James and Matthew first. In James I learned why we endure. How to grow. I also learned how to sow. In Matthew I got to know Jesus. What He done in all circumstances. How He loves. How He is there for others. How He reacted to good and bad people. I no longer just know of Him. I know Him intimately. My prayer is that this book will help you to understand and apply more of God's word in your life to break old ways and bring forth a new way.

Jill Deville

Many have been Christians for a long time. You will notice these Christian barely apply the word of God. They constantly stress, show anger, hate, judgement and control. I pray you grab your sword daily after this book. I pray it helps you to not feel defeated. God is not looking for quantity time with you. He is looking for quantity time with you.

Three months ago, I had my last brain surgery. It was one of three surgeries that took place in a ten-month span. I had began having pressure in my left eye and ear. I thought it was because of an earache, or just water in my ears. Then it got worse. I became dizzy. I had brain fog. I was dealing with headaches then pain in my body. I finally went to the doctor. They said nothing was wrong with my ears at all. They sent me to the ear specialist to see if it was something further inside going wrong with my ear. That apt checked out too. Nothing wrong, "they said".

My family doctor then sent me to the eye doctor. He said sometimes it is another thing infected or inflamed and it only appears to be the other things, in this case my ear. They tested my eyes and gave me glasses. They said, " that should do it". When the glasses came in, it felt like virtual reality. Everything moved with the glasses. I surely thought this is not what this is supposed to be like. I gave it time and patience. After a few weeks the symptoms of course was still there and now I was dealing with this weird eye glass situation. I made a new apt with the eye doctor. This time he checked behind my eye to see what was going on. That is when the issue was revealed.

It was showing I had extreme fluid building up in my brain. He then said I needed to immediately go to a specialist, and he set up the appointment. I then went to the appointment, and they did not take my insurance. They saw me of course and determined the exact same thing the other doctor did. I was not real sure why I had to even go to them for the same results. But now I was at a standstill. I could not do the treatment that was needed because they did not accept my insurance.

Throughout this time. I am praying, crying in prayer, and asking God to keep me safe and heal me. I never lost faith. I had decided to trust in Jesus with it all. The tears flowed but I stood firm. That devil wanted to defeat me. He knew if he could steal, kill, or at least destroy me. He would distract many others. But I had decided I was not allowing it. I hung on to the story I had read in Genesis about Joeseph. Genesis 50:19-20 in fact.

Genesis 50:19-20 NIV [19] But Joseph said to them, "Don't be afraid. Am I in the place of God? [20] You intended to harm me, but God intended it for good to accomplish what is now being done, the saving of many lives.

I decided if it worked for Joseph it was going to work for me. God would not have kept sharing that verse with me if it was not for me. This is why it is so important to know God's word. Within each circumstance you will hear some of the verses I shared with you in this book. Now you will hear them from God when you are in need or want. You can not hear Him as clearly and as loudly without knowing His word. It is like Jesus teaches us in Matthew we are what we eat.

Matthew 15: 17 NIV "Don't you see that whatever enters the mouth goes into the stomach and then out of the body?

If you are full of Jesus, when something comes up. Jesus will come out of you. If you are full of mess. Then mess will come out of you. We must learn we receive the armor and weapons from God. We also need to learn we must take the armor and weapons out the closet and put them on. We are not protected until we do. It does no good to just know we have it. We must put the armor on and use the weapons.

I was in too much discomfort, confusion, and concern. I did not want to distract the focus I needed. Therefore, I would pray and claim the scriptures that I included in this book. I would say them, until I believed them. I would say them through the waiting in the waiting room. I would say them while waiting for results. I would say them when waiting for the doctors to call me back. This is what gave me freedom and peace. What the devil meant to stress me, gave me peace. More peace that I had before knowing any of this was happening inside of me.

ARMOR UP

I went back to my family doctor, and he set up an appointment with a neurologist. He was great! The issue with all the doctors I was seeing, is that they were not aware of what was happening. They truly did not know what to do or what to tell me. BUT GOD DID. He worked through me. He worked through them. This happened because I decided to use my armor and weapon from God. The shield of faith, and the sword (word of God).

I prayed over them. I prayed for them to have ears to hear God, and to have hearts, minds, and hands to obey God. I did not call them stupid, selfish, inconsiderate. I decided they needed me just as much as I needed them. I decided God had gifted all of them with talents to work for Him. I decided if God assigned them to me then they could do it. That takes allot of faith. That takes allot of getting angry, concerned, upset but deciding not to sin in it. God's word teaches us; in your anger do not sin. Therefore, I assume in your stress, pain, whatever, do not sin. Focus on Him. So that was my goal.

The neurologist set me up for a procedure to release the fluid in my brain through a spinal tap. This was to get the excess fluid out. He done this to see if it would stay out or build back up. The pressure was over twenty-six cc's they took out. Anything over 30 is basically a stroke. Thank you, Jesus, for saving me is all I could say. I knew He had kept me through it all. I knew He is the only reason I did not have a stroke. I also know that if I did not have faith in Him and show that faith, I know I would have had that stroke. He showed me that with a few encounters.

This procedure is done with you awake and with numbing agents that hurt just as bad I think as the procedure to put in. During this entire process I said a list of scriptures that I included in chapter seven and eight for you. Saying, claiming, praying, and focusing on them helped my mind, mouth and motives stay in line with God. Once this was done of course I prayed not to have the symptoms that come with it and trust me; I did not. My God is faithful. They kept me on the medication that keeps the fluid from rebuilding to see what would happen next.

I felt great for a few weeks then I felt worse than before. I was once again pressing in deep not to sin in my wonder. I prayed and went to the doctor. The neurologist suggested I go to the ENT specialist to do a certain test. That was set up and I went. This doctor was great too. He done the test, saw the issue and set up the surgery. Again, through these tests, scans, blood work waiting, and wait times; I said, prayed, claimed, and focused on these scriptures. I knew that was the only weapons that would work. They were my promises from God.

In this surgery, they broke my nose and went into my face, nose, and brain and cleared out spurs throughout my cheek areas and all in there. They cleared out the nasal cavity and more. They put stents and then they packed it all up and woke me up. Let me tell you this is not a pleasant surgery or healing process. My nose still feels loose. I am told it takes time. Through the healing process I had to go through many stages and other procedures to clean, and then get the packing out.

Again, through it all no matter how much it hurt, or scared me. I would just say those scriptures and believe they were mind. I knew if I prayed what I was feeling it would not help. I knew if I said what I was feeling to others that surely would not help. Trust me the old unsaved or the old lazy Christian I used to would be, would be saying, "no, there is no way this works". I would have been mad, reserved, complaining, scared, and pitiful (devil weapons). I would have used every weapon the devil gave me thinking I could win with that dumb stuff. So, I get it if this sounds impossible or ridiculous. I was there before. But let me tell you this. Now that I have this type of faith. It is powerful, peaceful and it wins battles. Hard battles like this.

After this healing I was feeling great. The doctors kept me on the medication to watch what would happen with a goal to be taken off in six months if all was well. Guess what, in less than a month all was back again. I went back to the neurologist for my appointment, and he sent me to a specialist for neuro. He said at this facility they have special equipment to see in depth of your brain. Things that do not show in MRI, and all the other test that was ran with and without contrast. None of them were revealing the issue.

He set the appointment up and they called within a week and said to get over there. Now this specialist was known to be backed up for years not months. But instead of focusing on the facts, I decided only faith would win. And faith did win! I went to the appointment they ran test, and then we spoke about these test. I had veins in my brain that were nearly closed on each side. This was causing the fluid to build up and it needed to be opened to flow. He then set me up for a surgery to go in to put stents on each side to open the veins. Said it would be about an hour surgery.

Then there I went with the wonders again. Oh, my hair they going to have to shave my head and this recovery will be longer. I will not get back to work so quickly. I kept these wonders as thoughts I refused to claim them. I was enduring big time at this point. It was a lot to take in. I completely forgot this would heal the problem because I was looking at the process.

Many of us forget God's promises because we do not want to go through the process. We want the great nice home, but we do not want to work that much to pay for it or clean it. We want peace above all understanding, but we do not want to apply God's way, truth, and life to get to that peace. No matter what we must go through a process. It is the baptism of fire. If feels much like a fire burning under your butt, like you would see on the cartoons. It takes that fire to get us in motion. It takes that fire for us to take better care of ourselves. It takes that fire to get rid of the old stuff in us to have the new stuff birth through us. You can not get patience without dealing with people that will cause you to use that patience.

I went into this surgery and ended up in surgery for over five hours. During the surgery they discovered more of the veins in my brain were near closing and needed a balloon process ran throughout my entire brain. When I woke up, my head was not cut open, and my head was not shaved. They had gone in like an angiogram in 4 places in my arms and got to my brain with their unique operating tools. WHAT A MIGHTY GOD WE SERVE. Even in our silly prayers when you claim the scriptures and the promises that are yours. God searches your heart, and He makes powerful things happen. Things that help you never to forget. Also, things that will allow others to see when you take the invite and decide God can and God will heal this.

    We are not learning all this from the word of God not to use it. We do not lose the weight without the effort. We do not get the muscles without the effort. We do not get the degree without the effort. We will not get the access to this kind of miracles without the effort. We must believe to receive. We must understand believing is not seeing, believing is a process.

    The stents did not get to be put in because of the length of time it took to do the balloon throughout. When I woke up I knew who I was, I could talk, I could understand and this was all a miracle too. I did not need physical therapy of any kind and 2 days later I was at church praising my God for this miracle. The following week I was in my pjs, but I even preached. The miracle was so huge I do not think anyone noticed I had pjs on.

    I am healed better than ever now, and I am so grateful for this healing but also for the major spiritual healing within me during all of this. I am especially grateful for the miracle healing of all that witnessed God in this. I know they will apply this to their circumstance big or small because they saw what God can and will do right before their eyes. They also so what it took to access that healing was not easy, but it was grand.

    I pray this book encourages you to use your armor and weapons from God. They are so powerful. They will demolish strongholds. Know that your battles are never with flesh and blood. Your battle is always against the enemy. Your accountability is always with God only. Know that God has already promised you, that you can win. You just must be like David. You must have faith; you have to put on your armor, and you have to pick up that sling shot no matter how big that Giant is. Face it and win.

ABOUT THE AUTHOR

This book was written by Jill Deville. Jill is a country girl from Louisiana. Her greatest accomplishment is knowing Jesus and working for Him in her marriage, children, home, family, work, church, speaking events, and books. Jill strives to help people to know the word of God and how to apply the word of God in their lives. She has been with her husband for thirty years. Jill is a mother of three, one son, and two daughters. Her oldest children are married to their childhood sweethearts as well. Her youngest daughter is in eight grade and keeps her busy with band, and youth events. She is presently a grandmother of 3, they keep her heart filled with joy.

By profession, Jill is a Ten Year Certified LDP and Certified Mediator in the law field. She helps resolves family and civil matters in private. Her job fits her perfectly. God does say, " blessed are the peacemakers for they are children of God". She is also an Ordained Licensed Pastor of Gift Ministry of Louisiana a church she and her husband own and operate.

You can also stay connected and book events with Jill Deville on social media as Jill Deville World Ministry on all major social platforms. Her website is www.JillDevilleWorldMinistry.com.

Through this ministry she is a motivation speaker, publisher of her own books, teacher, and writer for sermons, bible studies, and bible classes. She travels for book signings, meet, and greets, women's conferences, writers' conferences, and even book clubs to interact with her readers. Most of all she loves to get to know her brothers and sisters in Christ. She loves to speak and teach about God. More importantly she reveals the simplicity in such a way that helps readers to know this is not about works, religion, or status. We learn the word of God to get to know Jesus as a Father and a Friend. Jesus taught with parables and direct simplicity. He taught her this and she can not wait to share it with you.

OTHER TITLES
Show What You Know

Show What You Know is inspired by James 1:22 where James teaches us that knowing the word of God is not enough, we must do it. Show What You Know was written to assist you to learn the word of God with simplicity like Jesus taught. Show What You Know will assist you on getting to know Jesus, not just knowing of Him.

Show What You Know will help you to trade old actions and reactions for freeing actions and reactions that will bring peace, joy, hope, love and so much more. Show What You know is great for new Christians that are wondering, "what now" and "how do I apply this" without feeling defeated on day 1. Show What You Know will help Christians get back to quality time with Jesus to break free from religious works or excuses.

Jesus has a plan for us to prosper and succeed and we do not want to miss our blessing because we just do not see them. Show What You Know is great for a Bible Study or to help you learn how to study because it constantly refers you to God's word.

Jill Deville

The Inheritance

Are you tired of sharing your promises, opportunities, trauma, drama, dreams, hopes (pearls) only to have them torn to pieces by family, friends, and enemies (pigs & dogs) ? Do the things you say tend to get exaggerated, or become the talk of the town? Do you hear things like " why do you want to do that" or "you should do this?"

This book will encourage you that Jesus believes in you, chose you, and is there for you with a resolution. Be encouraged that He is your best yes, provider, listener, healer, and protector! Jesus has so many promises (pearls) for you. The Inheritance will remind you how precious your pearls are and how to pass them on to have the best Inheritance to give.

THANK YOU

Thank you for your time, and support by reading the Armor Up. You truly are a blessing to God, and now to me tool. If you enjoyed this book, write a review; so that together we can reach more people for Christ.

If you would like to book an event, such as a women's conference, motivation speaking engagement for women, or teens, book signing/ meet & greet, or even a book club. Count me in. I would love to connect with you. I also travel to preach and teach the word of God too. Contact me at JillDevilleWorldMinistry@gmail.com

To stay connected look for Jill Deville, Show What You Know, and Jill Deville World Ministry on TikTok, Facebook, YouTube, & Instagram.

Know that you are loved and Already Chosen.
With all the love of the Lord,

Jill Deville

www.ingramcontent.com/pod-product-compliance
Lightning Source LLC
Chambersburg PA
CBHW032135040426
42449CB00005B/253